To the Chaplains in the Armed Forces with the prayerful good wishes of all in the Military Ordinariate.

† Francis J. Spellman, D.D.
† John F. O'Hara, C.S.C., D.D.
† William T. McCarty, C.S.C., D.D.
† William R. Arnold, D.D.

BOOKS BY FRANCIS J. SPELLMAN

No Greater Love
Action this Day
The Road to Victory
The Risen Soldier

Archbishop Spellman has given the rights
to this book to the New York Foundling
Hospital, which cares for children without
distinction of race, creed or color.

NO GREATER LOVE

No Greater Love

The Story of Our Soldiers

BY

FRANCIS J. SPELLMAN

Archbishop of New York

Military Vicar to the Armed Forces

NEW YORK

CHARLES SCRIBNER'S SONS

1945

It was my intention to dedicate this book to our American soldiers, our martyred dead, and the ideals for which they gave their lives.

As I was finishing this writing, Franklin Delano Roosevelt died, and I therefore dedicate this book to our boys and to their Commander-in-Chief, who, with them, fought and died to bring a just and enduring peace to their beloved America.

FRANCIS J. SPELLMAN

CONTENTS

NO GREATER LOVE

CHAPTER I

TEARS OF WAR

IN RECENT journeyings to the battlefields and the battle fronts of Europe, I met many thousands of our American soldiers who were fighting to achieve a victory and a peace whereby men may once again live as free men—freed from the yoke of hate and dark despair; freed from the fear of death. America's goal is not earthly gain, but the liberty of men and of nations and a just and enduring peace.

From the war, we have suffered deeply and grievously, but the pain and the pressure of America's anguish have been chiefly borne by our gallant boys, America's most precious possession, who have given their lives, their limbs, their eyes, and their health in an agony which endures most poignantly in the hearts of their beloved bereaved. But our cities and towns have not been reduced to gaunt skeletons and ashes nor have our homes been gored to death with gaping wounds. In nearly every other country at war, I have seen razed and carnaged cities; torn cathedrals; black ruins of homes melted into the ground, in mute mockery of man's faith and work and love.

This devastation in countries scourged by the savagery of war should make us gravely conscious of what might have been our own plight had we not been victorious, for even the ravages caused by the barbarian invasions of the past were insignificant in comparison with the desolation and chaos blanketing Europe today. In only a few months the heritage of centuries has been destroyed, a heritage not alone of material achievements but also of moral values. And deeply should we be moved to gratefulness to God and to those, our sons, who by their sufferings and sacrifices have spared America from bearing in her own body war's awful wounds.

Every nation, large or small, has its greatness and its glory, has its role in history, and its destiny. And America must never forget that, even after victory, she must fortify herself against the treacherous hatreds and cruelties that fester within conquering nations and burrow into the conquered. Hate and cruelty are contagious, and we must be on our guard lest we ourselves become contaminated with these diseases; lest, destroying one evil, we germinate and nurture another.

Before I left for Rome, I went to Washington to say good-bye to President Roosevelt. As always, his complete naturalness invited my sincere expression of opinion and frank exposition of facts, but no affability did or could make me forget that he was the President of the United States with a burden of responsibility so great as to surpass comprehension. We talked for an hour, and during our conversation we discussed the phrase "unconditional surrender." The President said that its meaning had been misinterpreted and distorted and he told me the familiar story of the origin of this phrase. It was, President Roosevelt explained, the expression that General Grant had used when General Lee asked him for terms of surrender. When Grant gave his ultimatum to Lee, the armies of the South were short of provisions; but it was still possible for them to continue fighting, as General Lee could have retreated into Carolina and there joined the armies of General Johnston. When Lee heard the phrase "unconditional surrender," he is reported to have said: "But my men, what about them? What about their horses? They own their horses, and they will need them for work on the farms." "We shall talk about that later," said General Grant, "but now, unconditional surrender." Lee capitulated, and Grant gave him more generous terms than he had expected, and the Southerners were permitted to keep their horses and side arms and were given provisions.

However, "unconditional surrender," in its modern interpretation, means something very different, both here and abroad. One nation that America is fighting had for her objective the domination of the world and the enslavement of mankind, and in her dictionary "unconditional surrender" means "annihilation." Germany's desperate propagandists have planted and cultivated in the minds of her people the belief that the Allies intend a Carthaginian peace and that Germany, like Carthage, will be destroyed. Thus the fanatical German leaders incited their people to fight to the last man and woman; to fight to the last bullet, and every foot of the way. For people who have no hope of life prefer to die fighting and killing others instead of merely being killed themselves.

The President explained that we had no intention of destroying the German nation and of killing or enslaving eighty million German people, and he left no doubt in my mind that he realized America's responsibility, as a victor nation, for an enduring world peace. The end we seek and the terms on which we rightly insist, he said, are those which will eliminate the possibility of Germany ever again becoming an aggressor nation. The Germans designing total victory must now endure total defeat!

We recalled that after the last war when Marshal Foch was criticized for not having marched on Berlin, he replied that the Allies had completely defeated the German Army and that the German generals were well aware of this. Beaten and broken, they had asked for an armistice. Foch estimated that if the armistice were refused and the fighting continued, the Allies might lose another fifty thousand lives, and he advised against such an unnecessary shedding of blood. The Allies could have imposed terms which would have insured the future security of France and Europe. That these hopes were not realized was due, not to the terms of the armistice, but to failure to enforce them. After the last war, the Germans denied that they had been defeated in a military sense; but after this war, with Berlin destroyed and occupied, with their cities shattered and their powers shackled, they will have no delusions!

Flying towards Rome several days later, these thoughts remained with me. Circling over New York's beautiful skyline, over LaGuardia Field and Whitestone Bridge, I thought, if all went well, it would be a long, eventful journey before I would again see that skyline. We flew over Long Island Sound and followed closely the Connecticut shore. We passed over Rhode Island, over Massachusetts near Boston, over Maine, the Bay of Fundy, and the Gulf of St. Lawrence. It was a beautiful flight, especially beautiful over forest-carpeted, lake-spotted Maine.

Arriving in Newfoundland just after sunset, we refueled and flew through the night, meeting the dawn just an hour or two before reaching the Azores. The plane was filled with passengers and by the time we arrived in Africa, through the usual "short snorter" ritual, I had become well acquainted with all aboard. I learned that we had passed through a severe storm, but I was still so behind in sleep that, strapped in my seat, I had slept through it all.

I was quartered in the Villa Maas, of Casablanca Conference fame, and early the next morning I left for Algiers, Naples and Rome. The trip along the North African coast had become almost a routine one for me, but it is always memory-stimulating, both for historical and religious reasons. In Algiers, Mr. Carmel Offie of the American State Department brought me the startling news that high German Army officers were attempting a revolt against Hitler. And again the words "unconditional surrender" fretted my mind. I realized that you cannot expect people to surrender when all they can look forward to is hanging, and I hoped that the revolt would bring new leaders into power with whom the Allies could make peace.

During the short stop-over in Algiers I had visited some wounded British soldiers who were being evacuated from the Italian fighting zone. Expeditiously yet tenderly, even in routine, they had been lifted from the plane and laid beneath the protecting shadow of its wings. Two of the most seriously wounded were placed immediately in an ambulance and hurried to the hospital. Others on the first lap of their journey home were awaiting transfer. It is difficult to know what to say to the wounded, who, outwardly calm, are generally introspective and confused by the shock of their experiences and the cascade of thoughts that tumbles through their minds. The spirit of courage with which they accept their plight and face the future is beyond understanding. They are strong, serene and brave. I thought of those at home who had no loved ones in danger and who themselves were spared from danger because millions of boys like these had paid dearly to protect and preserve them! When I attempted to sympathize with one boy on the loss of his leg he said simply and boldly, "I didn't lose it, Sir; I gave it." This was but one of a thousand deathless scenes I was to witness, as daily I sadly watched and prayerfully followed our own boys, as they departed upon missions from which there was no return. And vividly I recalled this English lad when another boy—it matters not his name, for his name is legion—volunteered to go on one of these death-dealing missions behind enemy lines. I heard his buddy say: "Johnny, that's a swell and brave thing to do, but *I* couldn't do it. Aren't you scared?" And I heard Johnny answer, not boast-fully, but calmly: "Scared? What for? What of? I'm straight with God . . . so what's there behind those enemy lines for me to be afraid of?" And to myself I whispered: "Dear God, such faith grant unto me."

Johnny went out—full of stout-hearted courage, sturdy in body, strong in spirit. He was brought back—his body broken, but his heart and spirit still stalwart and strong with the grace of God, though the sands of his life were running low. I said, as often and on many battlefronts with anguish I have said: "Johnny, I'm sorry you have to *pay* with your life." And he answered quietly, as the other boy had answered: "I'm not pay-ing, Father; I'm *giving!*"

That was "giving," in all its fulness, beauty and glory. But *we* shall never learn the lesson of this "giving" until the red heats of racial, religious and personal hates are melted white in the furnace of faith, blasting out and burning off the dross of selfishness, cruelty and lust. Only then will man regain his free-dom, happiness and peace.

Leaving Algiers Airport we flew fairly high over Algeria and Tunisia—about five thousand feet. At that height the only visible scars of war were the gaps where bridges over streams had been destroyed. War had passed here and peace had come, but it was a peace of loneliness and devastation. The towns were silent as tombs and were, actually, enormous tombs. And along the coun-tryside the sight of cemeteries brought memories of the dead buried in foreign soil, who still live enshrined in loving hearts and in God's glory. Is it not compellingly logical to believe that somewhere, somehow and in some way, there must be a balancing of the accounts of injustices, cruelties and heartbreaks? One of war's lessons must be faith in Eternal Life, otherwise life and death are empty, fruitless, and absurd, and sufferings and sacrifices vain and meaningless.

Over the modern ruins of Bone and Bizerte, close to the ancient ruins of Carthage, came memories of Augustine and Hannibal. Some of the things that now we see, both of them had seen, for both had walked along the same seashore. And one of the teachings of Augustine—"Suppress selfishness and spread charity"—is a warning as essential today to avoid future wars and as fundamental to future peace as it was fifteen centuries ago, if the peoples of all nations and all classes are to be united in justice and charity. For if men do not love justice, we shall not have peace.

From the air, even the stricken city of Bizerte did not seem unattractive, and distance helped also to soften the ugliness of the sunken ships in Bizerte's harbor. The Gulf of Bone was completely boatless and peacefully beautiful, with seven or eight flounces of surf edging its shores. Turning towards Sicily, only sky and sea were visible.

It was a dull, gray day and my feelings too were dull and gray as we passed over a barren edge of Sicily and reached the Italian coast near Salerno. Its shore was peaceful and deserted, but Salerno's peace had been dearly purchased, and the price of its quiet was the precious blood of American dead. I knew that, later, I should say Mass at Salerno's cemetery, but from the plane I breathed prayers that eternal repose had come to the valiant men whose youthful lifeblood had reddened those waters, beaches and hills. They had lived twenty-five years for D-day, and had died on that day's dawn!

Threading around the Sorrento Peninsula, we could see the

Amalfi Drive, Vesuvius, Capri and Naples! Naples, sparkling city of song and story, now lies haggard, battered and prostrate. "See Naples, and die!" is still a proverb, but today that proverb has a different meaning.

A short stop near Naples, at a pock-marked, cow-field-surfaced airport with shattered hangars and buildings and again we were in the air, northward bound, flying to Rome. We skirted the shore, passed Monte Circeo, Formia, Terracina and Gaeta, towns which even from the air we could see were in ruins. The sight of continuous ranges of mountains made me marvel, even more than I had marvelled at home, at the success of our armies in their march from Salerno. Even without the deadly hazard of enemy fire, the mountains seemed in themselves impassable. I remembered these mountains from my student days. I had walked around them and over the passes, and had visited villages and towns whose names today have taken on a new meaning. I could identify the sites of many of these towns that had survived centuries, but which now are merely places where towns once were. Monte Cavo appeared, dominating the Alban hills, and then Nettuno and Anzio, also reminiscent of years long past, places to which I had gone on excursions in happier days when a student in Rome. Pompeii, destroyed by the convulsive forces of nature, is not more bitten or flattened than are these towns demolished by the forces of man. No longer towns, they are names inscribed in blood and glory in the annals of American history. There were scenes both of regular and irregular devastation, large areas polka-dotted with shell craters, and sites of gun emplacements and bivouacs.

Familiar views rushed into vision so rapidly that my brain could not absorb the thoughts which pounded it. The Roman Campagna, the aqueducts, Castel Gandolfo, Lake Albano, and the dome of St. Peter's all rose before me and beneath me, and then all Rome swung around on a great turntable as the pilot made the air-circuit of the Eternal City. The winding Tiber and the bridges over the river, the Borghese Gardens, basilicas, forums and the Coliseum were as familiar as expressions on the face of a lifelong friend.

Landing at the airport from which long ago I had taken my first airplane flight, I was met by friends and driven into the city. The streets, last year deserted, were thronged. Old horse-drawn vehicles sagged lower. All the motor vehicles were military; camions, command cars, jeeps, and even the old green taxicabs had military designations over-painted on them. The Vatican cars and trucks had the gold-and-white colors of the Papal State. Soldiers were everywhere, and the signs in English on the hotels indicated that they had been requisitioned by the Allied armies. Rome seemed unreal. I had the sensation that I was witnessing a great drama. And I was. It was but one dolorous scene in a world tragedy.

I went at once to St. Peter's and then to the Papal Government Building, where I met Mr. Galeazzi, who has been my intimate friend for many years. I found him pale and worn, as surely he should be from the weight of troubles that oppress him, for he is charged with the great responsibility of the administration of the civil affairs of the Vatican. We went together to the American College Villa, where I had stayed in Rome the year before, and where I was to live during this visit. We talked until curfew and I learned for the first time that its literal meaning is "Cover the fire." And after curfew we still remained talking in the dark. We spoke much of the Holy Father, of his crosses, his occupations and preoccupations. We talked of Italy's tragedy and of the wretched plight to which her imprudent and impudent leaders had brought her. They had involved her in a war that was both foolish and wicked, a war which the people detested. The Italians were wedged between a force that compelled them to fight against us and a longing that urged them to join us. They found themselves in the distressing position of being in a war they did not wish to fight. This feeling was heightened by the fact that millions of Italians form a part of our people and are today true Americans, though they may have come to this country on the *Lusitania* or the *Roma,* and not on the *Mayflower.* Every nation has been mother and father to America, for America is the whole world in miniature, with men and women of all nations among her sons, and the blood in her veins, our heart's blood, is chaliced from the wounds of many peoples. And the Americans of Italian origin and descent did not hesitate to take up arms against their own brothers to defend their and our country.

It was almost dawn, and still we talked. Mr. Galeazzi told me of the terrible consequences of Italy's irresponsible act, which in the days to follow I was to witness in all their gravity and horror. Rimose mountain caves are homes for the homeless and hiding places for the hunted. Roads have been torn up and mined. Drainage systems of swamp lands have been destroyed and malaria has returned. Every energy necessary to life is lacking in Italy. Not a single railroad remains in order, not a train or any other means of travel or transport is functioning except for military uses. Flocks have been stolen and killed, men have been deported like herds of cattle, and families torn apart forever. Entire cities and towns have been reduced to rubble and ashes; churches and famous monuments are in ruins, whole regions have been sown with mines, and factories have been destroyed or sacked of every machine. There is a scarcity of the most indispensable objects, a lack of medicines and above all an extreme lack of food. This is the Italy of today!

Italy belongs to the Italians, but it belongs also to the whole civilized world; and if today America is to take its place in the first ranks in the struggle to maintain civilization, we Americans must feel that Italy is ours, because it is part of our civilization. If Italy is to be abandoned to destruction, a great part of all that renders the history of mankind beautiful will go into decay.

Daylight broke into our conversation and I left for St. Peter's, where I offered Mass at the Altar of the Chair of the Apostle, the altar at which I had been consecrated bishop twelve years ago.

During the morning I called on Myron Taylor, President Roosevelt's personal representative to the Vatican, and on Alexander Kirk, our Ambassador to Italy. I saw also several old Italian friends and found that war had traced its etching on them all. From them I learned much about what had taken place in Italy during the past months. After the armistice between the Allied Powers and Italy, the Germans had taken control of Rome and they ruled heavily and harshly. I heard the gruesome story of the massacre of the three hundred and twenty hostages, at the Tombe Ardeatine, in reprisal for the killing of thirty-two German soldiers by Italian patriots. I visited the catacombs, horrible scene of slaughter, and I talked with persons who were "nearest of kin" to two of the slain. Two priests were among the three hundred and twenty hostage-victims who were bound, machine-gunned and buried in quicklime. The building in which the execution took place was blown up to bury them. Heart-torn, tear-stricken mothers, wives and sisters of prisoners tried to find out whether their loved ones had been among these hostages, but the names of the massacred were kept secret for days so that all people with relatives in prison could be anguished. The mother of one of the executed boys gave me a photostat of the letter she had received notifying her that her son was dead, and that she might call for his clothing. Several persons told me of the torture house on the Via Tasso, where floors were wet with blood and tears. They asked me to visit this house of torture but I needed no further evidences of the atrocious scenes they had all too vividly described.

Shortly after my arrival in Rome I saw the Pope. This is always a deep emotional experience. It was afternoon, and the full light poured through the one window in his private office. The Holy Father was seated at his desk, with his chair backed to the wall. He arose and welcomed me with open arms. I felt almost as if I were seeing a vision, for the Pope, dressed in white, appeared to me like a figure from Tissot's famous picture, "Christ on the Waters."

In the course of my audience I found myself thinking back through the centuries, forgetting the passing of the years, renewing my faith and my hope, and I was startled as the thought, "Thou art Peter," broke through the veil of the present. The Pope had aged, thinned and saddened since last I had seen him. The past fifteen months had taken heavy toll. His is no robust physical stature nor has he strong, broad shoulders to bear the sorrows of the world. It is the spirit animating his body that gives him superhuman strength and endurance. War's slaughter, and its physical, mental and moral woundings, have left their indelible imprints on him. He suffers war's ever-intensifying, ever-increasing pressure and at times he feels crushed as its hatreds and cruelties spill torrents of human blood, saturate the world and sprout continuous crops of savageries.

The Holy Father's study is small, and near its window we

took chairs at right angles to each other. His full face, turned towards me in the afternoon light, seemed alabaster. Beyond him I could see his desk with five stacks of papers neatly arranged on it, and near the desk was the typewriter at which he himself composes and writes all his important letters and addresses. The Pope did most of the talking. I wish his words could sound in the ears of all the war-stunned, war-deafened people of the world, could reach the brains and pierce the hearts of men hardened in the crucible of war. Thus the fruits of all the pains and agonies of broken minds and broken hearts might be an enduring peace on earth. The right of a nation to live was, he said, as sacred as the right of the individual; but the will of one nation to live must never become the death sentence for another nation. This supreme and indestructible truth must prevail at the peace table if the peace itself is not to be the vestibule to another war. Explicitly and courageously, the Holy Father denounced the errors and abuses of the totalitarian systems. He said that it had not been possible for him to take any practical initiative towards peace, because the belligerents were not united even in wishing to hear mention of the word "peace," but that he himself will leave nothing undone to lessen misery and hasten an impartial and lasting peace. He has ever maintained that the guilt of beginning and prolonging a war was no graver than that of making an unjust or breakable peace.

The amassed ruins, the spilled blood, the tears of war have made it all too sadly evident that religion of itself, un-lived, will not make or keep peace. Religion to be effective must be lived and practiced, and not alone by the few but by the multitude. It is not a cloak to be worn or doffed on occasion. It must be an all-penetrating, permeating spirit. It is active love of God and of one's fellowmen and it is this universal spirit that is fundamental to world peace. Nations and families, large or small, must learn to live together in understanding and tolerance, in mutual forbearance and charity. It may be that the millennium will never dawn, but if the future is always to be dark the responsibility and the fault lie in man's own perversity, man's hardness of head and heart, man's blindness, bitterness, and selfishness. If the spirit of charity and mutual respect cannot make men agree on fundamentals and essentials, their own self-interest, it would seem, should be enough to maintain concord. If the leaders of men *want* peace, the Pope concluded, let them ponder before God the justice of their demands so that what they decide will be fair to both victors and vanquished. Otherwise, in the terms of their pacts will be hidden the seeds of new wars.

As I took my leave, I realized the burden of the Pope's weight of sorrow and his thirst to bring peace on earth, but I realized too that "the morrow of victory has more perils than its eve."

CHAPTER II

A NATION'S AGONY

WHILE in Rome fifteen months ago, I had seen nothing of the city, for I had remained in the American College Villa except for the occasions of my visits to the Vatican. It was a long-awaited experience to be able to go about the city again. In former days groups of seminarians had been familiar sights, and their nationalities were identifiable by the varicolored cassocks and sashes they wore. Americans wore the usual flat, beehive-shaped hats, and black cassocks flashed with sky-blue bands and buttons, and wide red sashes. These were soldiers in God's army. Now, the Americans who walk the streets of Rome are khaki-clad, with varicolored shoulder patches. They are soldiers in another army. In other years American students were not permitted the luxury of riding in horse-drawn or motor-driven vehicles. They were required to walk to and from the University every class day, and on free days to and from the museums and other places of interest. In Rome, today, the few taxis and horse-drawn vehicles have American soldiers as their chief patronage.

In the beginning of the occupation, the Romans received the Americans as liberators. They acclaimed them with flowers, with joy and with gratitude. This first enthusiasm was dulled when we did not do everything that the Italians had expected. For the most part, though Americans had good will for the Italians, it was impossible for Americans to forget that Italy had declared and waged war on the United States and that Italy was a defeated nation. The Italians themselves realized to the full that they had been defeated, but they had expected that the transition from enemy status through "co-belligerency" to that of full allies would be more rapid. Their defeat has left them sad and dejected. Disillusioned, stunned and completely crushed, the Italians now ask only the right to work to gain their daily bread. They need our help to help themselves. Even though the Four Freedoms are emblazoned on the American-printed Italian currency which the Italian Government is obligated to honor, they do not mean the same thing to the Italians that they mean to us. Few people in Italy know "Freedom from Want," and there are fewer still who have "Freedom from Fear."

I heard a story about an over-zealous American officer who, being able to recite the Four Freedoms from memory, and determined to do everything in his power to spread his interpretation of them, walked into the chapel of a hospital which had been requisitioned by American forces. The officer decided to remove the crucifix, and was in the process of doing so, when another officer remonstrated with him, only to hear the retort: "Ain't we fighting this war for the freedom of religion?" If freedom of religion is to be interpreted as being freedom to undermine and destroy religion and tear it from the hearts and lives of men, then, even while wearing the aureole of victory, we are in a sorry plight. I hope that the Allies will respect the religion of the people of Italy, who are, according to various estimates, from ninety to ninety-nine percent Catholic. Both the British and the American forces respected the Moslem religion when they occupied Arab countries, and one never heard of mosques being requisitioned. I recall an observation made to me by a Moslem. Smilingly he said something from which no smile could take away the sting: "God must love the Moslems, for you Christians kill one another."

The solution to the confused and clouded Italian problem
does not rest with the Allies alone. There are internal problems
and the greatest one is disunity among the Italians themselves.
We in the United States have our own particular differences,
but we are one in fundamentals and essentials. We have diver-
gences of opinion and of interests. We differ in racial origins,
but we are one in patriotic devotion to the welfare of our country, the prosperity of our countrymen, and in the safeguarding
of the rights of our minorities. In Italy and in other liberated
countries, the discords are so many and so deep, that peace will
not come to them until democratic governments have been
established with the essential safeguard of all true democracies,
the protection of the rights and liberties of all citizens.

In Rome I met a cab driver whom I had known for many
years, and we talked about America. I explained our form of
government and asked him what he thought about democracy.
He said, "If democracy will get me work and keep me from
starving, I'm for it, but democracy isn't here yet, and I don't
think peace will come until long after the duration! If both the
Allies and the Italians would spend more time in getting food
to the people who are hungry," he added, "work for the people
who are idle, and less time finding out what year someone was
enrolled in the Fascist Party, things would be much better for
every one in every way." Though I talked with many other persons of all classes, from the "man in the street" to the man in
administration, and heard their versions and aversions, no man
expressed himself more clearly or succinctly!

Rome depends completely for its food on the surrounding
countryside, and within the city many Romans of all classes
are suffering from hunger. Thirteen years ago I had been a
frequent guest at the home of a Roman family and because of

our friendship I wished to visit them. I realized that to have me at their table might cause them embarrassment, but I felt it would be a greater embarrassment if I declined the invitation. During the evening the family told me that they had done everything possible and gone to many places trying to get a chicken for supper. They did not find a chicken, but through a great favor they did succeed in getting a rabbit. For me, there was an additional but undisclosed hardship in eating that rabbit! They told me of the great suffering caused by inflation, for the lira has depreciated in value from four cents to one and in the black market the currency is even more depreciated. This is bitterly demoralizing, for it is maddening to work hard and still be unable to buy enough food to keep one's self or one's family from hunger. An Italian who receives a dollar, or one hundred lire, a day for his work is very fortunate; yet one hundred lire buys only five potatoes, a loaf of bread and five lumps of coal. In Rome an egg costs forty cents—if one can find an egg!

I welcomed every opportunity to see and to learn, for and by myself, about conditions in Italy. The major problems are food, clothing and work. Hundreds of thousands of people are homeless, hungry, sick and ill-clad. During the days I walked about Rome, I met old friends in new surroundings and saw new faces amid old scenes. All I met were depressed; all I saw and heard was depressing. The horrors and terrors of the past, the sufferings of the present and the fears for the future possessed and oppressed them. No family and no person had been left untouched. The Germans had not only devised new techniques of killing but at all times kept plentiful reserves of civilian hostages available for instant reprisals, and no one knew when he or some member of his family would be one of these innocent victims.

One day I attended an audience which the Pope grants every day at noon to Allied soldiers. When our armies first reached Rome, arrangements for these audiences were made through military and diplomatic channels, and placings were assigned according to military rank. Thus, only officers were near the Pope when he spoke. Observing this, I felt that in the house of him whose home is home to all mankind, there should be no distinction made between field marshal and private soldier. When I told this to the Holy Father, he at once agreed and said, "The only pass required is any uniform." And now these audiences are unique, for here generals and G.I. Joes of all nationalities are grouped together, shoulder to shoulder. The Pope usually speaks in three languages, for there are always present soldiers from the British Commonwealth of Nations, America, France and Poland. He passes among them, blesses all the religious articles they bring; and every one is amazed to see him, of all the great men of the world, the only one totally unguarded and unprotected. At one of these audiences, an American soldier gave the Holy Father the mahogany head of an angel that he had picked up in the ruins of Monte Cassino; and another, having read that there was no chocolate in Italy, brought him a dozen chocolate bars!

Boys who came back to Rome from the forward lines enjoyed the experience because Rome was in marked contrast to the many villages, towns and cities that they had seen destroyed. Many organizations strove to make the soldiers feel at home. Sightseeing tours were arranged and many opportunities provided for rest and recreation. The men ate their meals seated on real chairs, at tables with tablecloths, in a "homey" atmosphere; and in Rome, unlike many other places, it was not necessary to place the legs of the tables in tin cans filled with water so that ants couldn't climb up the table! The boys wrote their letters home at

charge was that he was a Fascist. He was a victim of "epuration"
as the process of "defascising" is called. Its theory is to bring to
justice those who have been responsible for the tyrannization of
others or who have collaborated with the enemy. This seizure
of collaborationists and suspected collaborationists was widespread, and the failure to separate the guilty from the innocent
was charged with agony. The danger in epuration is that it can be
used for personal vengeful purposes against innocent people.
The prisoner that I visited claimed that he had always been a
patriotic citizen, was a veteran of the first World War and his
brother, an American, was serving in the United States Navy.
It was a typically tragic topsy-turvy example of what happens
in wartime.

Fires of hate burning in human hearts burst, blaze and break
into mass conflagration. Violence is born out of such hatreds,
as in the case of a mother who wished to see her own son dead
in order to cause pain to his wife. Thus may nations hate one
another, even to their own destruction. Ernie Pyle said he could
not stand the sight of another dead man, or hear the burst of
another bomb; and it is hard for me to bear the story of another
broken heart, the tragedy of another broken home, or the despair
of another broken nation.

Many are the recriminations against the Italians. Their par-
ticipation in the war against the Allies prolonged the strife
and cost hundreds of thousands of casualties. Many Italians
wished to vindicate themselves and redeem the country by taking
active part in the war, but in the beginning Allied strategy did
not permit this. Although the Italians, called co-belligerents, are
not allies, the United States faces a decision of immediate and
long-term consequence in relation to Italy and to the world. In
accepting her humanitarian responsibilities the United States is

creating and implementing a program for alleviating the impend-
ing starvation and economic prostration of a vanquished and
penitent people. Otherwise, Italy, abandoned to civil disorders
and famine, will again become the prey and the prize of totalitarian forces.

The economic devastation in Italy is almost total. Few people
outside the country or even the Italians themselves—and I have
talked to hundreds of them—can conceive the death-blow that
has been dealt the Italian economy. The wanton scorched-earth
tactics of the German Army have caused one of the greatest
tragedies of this war. And I have seen this tragedy.

The deliberate mining of power and industrial plants, the
bombing of bridges and strategic rail-centers, the systematic
flooding of vast land-reclamation projects, the expert demolition
of port facilities and communications, the looting and levelling of
homes, these have set Italy back a century.

The meagre quantity and poor quality of the national diet
have caused widespread hunger, disease and moral degeneration.
Information from an official Allied source revealed recently that
many thousands of girls between the ages of ten and twelve
were being treated in Naples hospitals for diseases that came
from selling their bodies for bread. The answer to most of Italy's
human needs is more food, and the answer to Italy's economic
needs is transportation. Most of the Italian main railway lines
were electrified, and the situation regarding electric power in
liberated Italy is desperate. The systematic demolition of railroad bridges, roadbeds, and marshalling yards has curtailed traffic movements drastically, and has added to the root economic
obstacle to Italy's comeback. "The Poor Earth" cannot produce
enough food or raw materials to sustain her. Moreover, Italy has
been ransacked of useful implements and machinery, and has

been forced back into primitive types of handicraft and agriculture. The world-clock has ticked backwards a hundred years.

Another affliction of Italy is its black market. This illicit trading seeks out the highest bidders, not buyers, encourages hoarding of essential commodities and creates strong inflationary trends. Wage levels and price structure present a woeful disparity, so that the devaluation of the Italian currency has worked its greatest injustices on the middle and lower classes.

Medicines are in short supply and lack of clothing still further aggravates deaths. The tubercular death rate is rising rapidly and infant mortality has sharply increased, one out of every three children dying in its first year. I saw thousands of homeless and helpless living in the fields, under bridges, in barns and barracks, and within the shells of devastated buildings.

Twenty-two years of Fascist domination and the war years under the Nazi heel have left the Italian people discouraged, cynical, confused. Have you ever watched the agony of a person you loved? It is an anguishing experience, but this feeling is multiplied a thousandfold when one watches the agony of a nation.

The Allied occupation of Italy can aggravate or ameliorate the problems of post-war adjustment. It can set a pattern for peace that may breed good-will or hatred. We cannot afford to make an ersatz peace. Italy cannot be amputated from the European economy; nor can she be sliced up as fair loot. Italy has a surplus of highly efficient technicians to help in her own reconstruction if she has the material and tools, and then she can take her place and pay her share among the nations of the world. Italy has the head, heart and hands to rebuild her economic structure if given a chance. She knows she must make her come-back the hard way, but in clearing away the wreckage strewn by Fascism and the war, the road back must not lead to economic and political ruin, making Italy a land of beggars, a land of slavery and a land of slaves.

The uprising of the hungry and the unemployed would mean a sweeping victory for Godless government, and the peace will be lost even as the war is won. Those who have seen Italy lying in blood and ruins from south to north, those who have seen her overturned cities, her crumbled glorious monuments, her homeless, shelterless, starving, sick and dying people, cannot forget the picture and, remembering it, cannot remain heart-hardened or dry-eyed.

CHAPTER III

WRITTEN IN AMERICAN BLOOD

I FLEW north to General Clark's headquarters and received the warmest of welcomes from the valiant soldierly commander of America's Fifth Army and from his efficient and energetic Chief of Staff, Major General Alfred M. Gruenther. In the sixteen months that had elapsed since I had seen them in North Africa, the Fifth Army had traveled a long, difficult, bitter road to the Arno River. The Army itself seemed to partake of the personality of General Clark. Rugged, indomitable in spirit and in power, it had gone onwards in the attainment of most difficult objectives.

General Clark is a soldier, but he is also a man, a husband and a father. He is conscious of his responsibility to his country, to his men and to the future. Tall, straight and sturdy as a young oak, he is as quick-moving as a panther. Resourceful and determined, he places great emphasis on training, in which he stresses three points: discipline, physical conditioning and realistic battle environment. "Thus," he said, "my men have better chances to survive."

The General works hard himself and demands hard, intelligent work of others. Equipped with an extraordinary memory, he is a master of detail. He knows at all times the location of every unit in his command and is completely intolerant of carelessness, because carelessness costs lives. His emphasis on training, together with his military ability, made it possible for the Fifth Army to pass through the hitherto impregnable defensive peaks of southern and central Italy to liberate Rome and bring freedom to Italy.

General Clark brought General Gruenther and myself to his van, where we had a half-hour's talk before luncheon. They were just as eager to learn of America at home as I was to learn of America on the battle front. Many months of war had made the Fifth Army the equal of any army of professional soldiers in the world. His men, the General said, were "strong, brave and united" and I wish that Americans at home could have heard the note of pride in his voice as an inspiration for unity at home. General Clark's van, a new one, was a surprise gift from his staff. I had the privilege of using his old van, which is indeed historic, for he had used it on the way from Salerno to Cassino and northwards during the most trying days of the Italian campaign.

Wishing to visit as many units as possible, I left immediately after luncheon and went to an evacuation hospital about an hour's ride from headquarters, where I met the personnel and the patients. Ambulances with their precious freight of wounded soldiers were being brought to the hospital. Some of them had been wounded in combat only an hour previously, and they told me they had been picked up almost as soon as they had been hit. Quickly, but with unhurried efficiency, the wounded were given blood plasma, treated for shock and X-rayed. The X-ray picture was ready in a few moments, and together with the history and diagnosis, went with the patient into the operating tent. Prayerfully, I followed each single one as he was borne away to be operated on by some one of our country's ablest surgeons. It was consoling to me to see the treatment and the care given to our soldiers, so prompt and adequate that there are few fatalities among the wounded men who live to reach evacuation hospitals. One boy, badly shot up, nearly unconscious and in pain, remembered I had confirmed him back in the United States. He struggled to say to me: "Thank you, Father, for coming to see me"—and these words, though I have heard them again and again, always make my whole trip worthwhile, no matter how distant or how difficult the journey.

All services in the Army are co-ordinated in a manner that to me is amazing. I have followed the processes of the induction and training of soldiers, the provision of food, the manufacture of equipment and ordnance, and the transportation system that covers the world, bringing men and everything they use to the right place at the right time. It is a gigantic task and a fantastic operation. The lucky Fifth Army soldiers always had their food on time, even on the march, and they nicknamed their quartermaster, General "Never-Lost-a-Meal" Sullivan. How essential is this co-ordination to success was explained to me by General Clark. Air Forces, Infantry, Airborne Troops, Artillery, and other combat units, must be perfectly integrated in action. If the photographers do not get good pictures, the operations of the Air Force are hampered; if the Signal Corps does not function perfectly, the communications go awry; if the engineers do not promptly reconstruct blown bridges, and sweep mines from fields and roads at great peril to themselves, then the whole mechanism of the Army's smooth functioning is hampered and handicapped.

We drove back to General Clark's headquarters where we had one of our "Sullivan suppers," and afterwards the General and I took a walk in the pine grove along the shores of the Tyrrhenian Sea. The General is so tall and takes such long strides that the only way in which I could keep up with him was to take two steps to his one, but I had some consolation in the fact that his black spaniel dog called "Pal" had to take even more steps than I did to cover the ground. General Clark's dog is "Pal" in fact as well as in name, and when possible the General himself assumes the responsibility of feeding him, insisting that "Pal" have vegetables mixed with his meat, but, he said, "Pal" prefers meat without vegetables!

We did not go near the water, for the General warned me that it was dangerous to walk in places that had not been mineswept, and just the previous day a soldier who had been ten months in combat had gone to a rest area, went in swimming, stepped on a mine, and was killed. Death seemed to be around every corner every minute and even broke into the quiet of our walk, when General Clark's aide came to us and said, "General McNair was killed today in France." General Clark was visibly affected. He told me that he had been General McNair's Chief of Staff, that he greatly admired him, and that the Army would miss him.

That was an unforgettable hour with General Clark, away from the bivouac area, with umbrella pines above and a pine-needle carpet beneath us. With the red of the sunset and the song of the crickets, we had a moment's illusion of being in a world of peace, but suddenly in our pathway there were three white crosses and the graves were those of German soldiers.

The next morning, I left headquarters to say Mass in the field for the 85th Division. Over five thousand soldiers were present. General John B. Coulter and General Geoffrey Keyes were there at the Mass, and for me, and I am sure for all the others, the occasion was memorable. Many times and almost constantly for many months these combat soldiers had been in serious danger. They were battle-hardened and battle-wise. Yet their devotion was childlike and for over an hour they knelt in the blazing sun in the dust of the field.

Later, I went to the Fourth Corps to meet an outstanding American Army unit under the command of General Crittenberger. I met all of the General's staff, including Major Henry Cabot Lodge, Jr., former United States Senator from Massachusetts, and talked both with officers and enlisted men. General Crittenberger was gracious enough to give me a map detailing the advances of the Corps, on which he wrote: "This record of accomplishment is inscribed as a souvenir of the Fourth Corps and in grateful appreciation of the strength and inspiration which your visit gave us." This map, with its inscription, is a precious keepsake and I shall always remember General Crittenberger's expression as he presented the map and pointed out the march: "That line was written in American blood."

The next day, we went to visit the Second Corps and the Eighty-eighth Division. We used a sedan as far as road conditions would permit, but a long distance had to be covered in a jeep, and the Chaplain's jeep was named "Bringing Up Father." The road was very rough and the dust was very thick. I had been told both of the roughness and the dust and had been advised to wear a G.I. uniform. And I did. I was thankful for this suggestion, for otherwise I should have been a mighty sorry sight after the dusting and jouncing I received. The dust was so thick that it rolled off the windshield in dust-drops. Somewhere along the journey some one gave me a dust mask. It was a great relief.

With Monsignor Chataignon, one of the great chaplains of the war, I finally reached the command post of General John P. Sloan, who brought me forward to the 351st Infantry. General Sloan, now one of General Clark's division commanders, had been one of his professors, and General Clark smilingly told him that if things went wrong he would blame it on his teacher. The men were living in dugouts, foxholes and huts. They were on the river side of the last range of hills rolling down to the Arno River, the dividing line of No Man's Land. I met men who went daily on patrol duty into enemy territory. General Sloan told me how costly would be those yards between our lines and the river, and the yards on the other side of the river to the mountains.

General Keyes, General Sloan and other generals whom I met were kind enough to give me shoulder patches from their outfits, and if I continue to gather insignia I shall have as many colors for my shoulders as Joseph had for his coat.

I was permitted to make a flight out over the Arno River near Pisa to land in Leghorn. I flew in a small Cub plane. While we were close to enemy lines there was little or no danger of being shot down, for it is not profitable to knock down such a small plane at the cost of revealing gun locations which almost immediately become subject to accurate and concentrated artillery fire.

Leghorn had been very badly demolished. I went through its desolate, deserted streets in the downtown business and dock area, and saw the extensive irreparable damage. After seeing the desolation of Leghorn and of other flattened cities it is easy for me to credit the statement that Italy has been ruined for a hundred years. One gets accustomed, and at the same time one gets sick, witnessing war's destruction.

During my days with the Fifth Army, King George VI came to see us. He was accompanied by General Sir Harold Alexander, Commander-in-Chief of the Allied armies in Italy. The King received a most cordial welcome and reviewed the American troops. He walked from one end to the other of the mile-long line of soldiers and paused many times to say a word of greeting and congratulation to individuals and units. His Field Marshal's uniform bore the Royal Air Force insignia over the left breast pocket, for King George has earned his rating as a a pilot.

Just before we sat down to luncheon there was a heavy explosion. General Clark told us it was a mine, and as the smoke belched upwards I recited the form of absolution, for it was almost certain that some one was dying or killed. The soldier who had stepped on the mine had been fatally wounded, and in a short time was dead.

King George is a very natural, cordial person of average height and figure. His light-blue eyes are friendly and he seems to bear very well his responsibilities as King and Emperor of approximately one-quarter of the world's population.

The King stressed the necessity of maintaining unity between America and England, not only as essential to victory but also as fundamental to world peace. This, I know, is America's aim. America's power has been dug out of the earth by the labor and skill of her people; and her victories, her independence and her prosperity have been earned by their industry, their valor and their brains. It will be tragic if our dearly bought military victories do not bear fruit worthy of our sacrifices. We believe that the goal and reward of victory must be the absolute safeguarding of our own freedom and the extension of help and the granting of freedom to other men and nations. However, those who strive to stem with their lives the torrents of hatred, cruelties and killings that threaten to break through the dykes of civilization must sometimes feel like the famous little Dutch boy.

When the King asked General Clark how old he was, they found they were both forty-eight. General Gruenther is forty-five, and when General Alexander, General Keyes and General Crittenberger told their ages, I discovered that I was the oldest one at the table. Probably, I shall soon be forced into military retirement! General Alexander has not a gray hair in his head, and looks very young. He is so soft-spoken in manner that it is difficult to think of him as the commander of all the armies on the entire Italian front.

After my days with the Fifth Army, I returned to Rome, and had several audiences with the Pope. Talking in the quiet of his private study with its simple classical ivory crucifix on the wall above him, and a delicate porcelain statue of the Pieta in a niche opposite him, it seemed a far cry from the violences of war from which I had just returned. And yet the war is closer to no one, and no one feels closer to the war than the Pope. Not only has he been endangered by the many bombings, but he himself has gone out into the midst of them, gone to the dead, the dying, and the bereaved, wanting to share in the sorrows of his people.

Nightly, after our talks, I would go with the Pope to his chapel with its baldachin altar, similar in style to the main altar in St. Patrick's Cathedral in New York. The simple silver tabernacle, a temple in miniature, has graceful little columns of black marble and a tiny dome resembling that of St. Peter's. On the green drapery behind the altar is embroidered the Sacred Heart, and on the left is a life-sized painted statue of Our Lady and Child carved in wood. The Stations of the Cross are also of carved wood in silver frames. The Holy Water font, exquisitely combining glass and silver, represents the Samaritan woman at the well.

Pius XII's influence is felt within his rooms, not because his symbolic coat of arms decorates the walls, but because of his own personality. The things he keeps near him are eloquent of his whole life. The personal furnishings in his bedroom, study and chapel mark the stages of his career, and, together with many objects given to him and dear to him, recall chapters in his life.

While in Rome, I called on the former Premier of Italy, Victor Emmanuel Orlando, one of the Big Four at Versailles, and its only survivor. Short, compact in build, he bristles with energy despite his seventy-five years. His step is quick and sure, his skin, clear and healthy, and his head is covered with silver hair worn pompadour. The only signs of age are the pockets beneath his small, grayish-blue eyes. Smilingly he referred to his age and said that he had his bag packed for his final journey, and was ready to face his Eternal Judge. When I told him I was moved by his buoyancy of spirit despite his years and the afflictions of his beloved Italy, he replied that he could not afford the luxury of showing sadness.

He talked of the work he had tried to do for his country, a work which, with the prostration of Italy, he now sorrowfully sees in ruin. Speaking of the excesses of "epuration," and its concomitant evils, the Premier said that epuration had also eliminated many of the industrial and professional leaders of the land, and that a country without leaders was a country without hope. It is always a difficult and dangerous operation to try to eliminate all the evil and yet retain all the good. It is not as simple as the operation which confronts a surgeon with an encapsulated tumor which he can cut out without harming healthy tissue.

Orlando graciously insisted on walking with me to the

automobile to bid me good-bye and was deeply impressed by the tiny car with its plate on the door indicating that it was the one the Pope had used when he visited the thousands of victims in the stricken San Lorenzo district.

I was also invited to call on Prince Umberto, who lives and has his offices in the Quirinal Palace. I stayed with him for half an hour and we naturally talked of Italy's past and present passion. In spite of the many factors and factions against him, Umberto, in his anomalous position, seems to be doing everything that he can to unite and sustain his divided, discouraged, dispersed people. Dressed in civilian clothes, he seemed more like a businessman than a monarch. Tall and slender, he did not appear much older than when last I had met him on the day of his wedding.

Hour by hour and day by day, I heard the same litany of sorrows, despairs and hopes against hope, from the high, the lowly and the in-between. It was the same story I heard from Premier Bonomi, the man who had been Prime Minister of Italy before Mussolini, and who again had been summoned in his elderly years to assume the almost impossible responsibility of heading the government of six parties. Premier Bonomi's lifetime of integrity, his intense desire to do everything to co-operate with the Allies in reconstructing Italy are factors helpful to him in this gigantic task. He knew that the armistice terms were very hard, that Italy was still only partially liberated, that even in the freed regions there was disunity and despair. But beneath that burden he strove, encouraged by hope and by his belief in the assurance of the Allies that the armistice would be modified in Italy's favor if she aided the United Nations during the remainder of the war. And bravely he pleaded that Italy share the shedding of blood for her own redemption.

I was able to fulfill my desire to pay tribute and say prayers at the cemetery in Anzio which has become sacred American soil. I offered Mass at an altar erected over the grave of Father Joseph Gilmore, a chaplain from the Archdiocese of New York. In the distance are the Alban hills, and the cemetery, framed with elms, is located not far from the sea in a flat area surrounded by gentle slopes covered with groves of olive trees. A freshly painted flag-pole with its brand-new American flag stands in the center of the plot—a sentinel honoring those men who have given their lives to and for America.

Father Gilmore had been in the Anzio area only a short time and was a chaplain in reserve awaiting assignment in the place of any priest on regular duty who might be killed. In charge of the hospital reception unit, he went long periods without sleep that he might be with every wounded patient as soon as he was brought to the hospital. When finally overcome with exhaustion, he cautioned medical soldiers on duty to wake him whenever a seriously injured man was brought in from the field. One night, when Father Gilmore was attending patients in the admission tent, the medical installation was bombed and strafed. He was anointing a soldier, when the Germans came again and dropped their bombs. Father Gilmore and a number of soldiers were killed instantly. His Colonel tried to locate a priest, but it was not until some hours later that Father Kennedy was able to get there. Father Gilmore's soldiers had whispered the act of contrition in his ear and prayed by his side long after his death. In the midst of this field of white crosses and stars, I prayed for peace with the deepest realization of the priceless cost of war.

Flying away from Italy, the happiness of being there because of its memories was counterbalanced by the realization that those

memories are now specters of the past. We were over Monte
Cassino, not only a dead city but a city of the dead. Amid the
gaunt shells of its broken buildings are the broken bodies of
countless men, and the odor of rotting, pulverized flesh adds
to its horror. Cassino is a valley of death, and through this valley death still stalks, for there are an estimated half-million
mines mixed in the ruins. I saw these mines everywhere—piles
of them, flat and round, heaps of potato-masher grenades, and
stacks of rusty, fin-tailed mortar shells. Cassino is the world's
Gethsemane. I heard the story of its agony from our men who
struggled, suffered, and destroyed Cassino, and left buried in its
tomb their own beloved dead. Before me I could still see the
face of the saintly old Abbot of Monte Cassino, nor shall I ever
forget the anguish in his voice as he told me of his trek from
the sepulchre of the monastery into the open rainfall of bombs,
holding his crucifix before his eyes, and to me he whispered:
"All that I have left are my eyes with which to cry."

Memories of Monte Cassino blended into memories of other
years as I flew away from Rome with General Tom Darcy—
passing high over the Lake of Bracciano, skirting the Italian coast
and crossing the Tyrrhenian Sea, to Corsica. I had stayed with
Tom when I was in North Africa during the last days of the
historic advance of the British Eighth Army and the American
9th Air Force from El Alamein to Tunis. In Corsica I visited
many American outfits, veterans of that campaign. The additional year of war had wrought great changes in the attitude of
many of these men. They were definitely more hardened, more
casual, more determined and more confident. Their long successful advance along the entire North African coast to Sicily, Italy
and Corsica had been triumphant but costly. Most of them spoke
of places they had bombed, of victories they had won, with the

same intonation with which young men of their ages formerly used to talk about their ball games and other competitive sports. War, too, is a game—but the score is counted in human lives and written in human blood.

Hardships and sufferings of every kind—cold, heat, mud, sand, hunger and sickness, riding always with death—had given these men a disregard for life, even for their own. They were less concerned about themselves and their own injuries and sufferings than about the worries and griefs of their home folks. In one hospital, I visited a boy who had recently lost his right leg. He had written to his mother saying he was in the hospital to "avoid infection." He wanted to spare her sorrow, and himself pity, until his return to the United States, when it would no longer be possible to avoid telling her the whole truth. Some lads who had been wounded more than once told me frankly that they did not want to return to the front lines because they felt they had done their share, and that others should take up and carry on the fight.

Yet there were some who could not wait to get better, so impatient were they to return to combat. One of these was a boy from Michigan, who had become a legend in his outfit. He had been brought back unconscious from the front lines, not wounded, but actually sick from exhaustion. The doctors bedded him down in the hospital—but the next morning he was gone. That evening he was brought in again—only to be gone once more in the morning! When he was brought back that night, the doctors tried a new "treatment," and threatened to send him home if he did not stay abed until he recovered his full strength. Possibly this "treatment" cured him, for at least he was not again brought back to that hospital!

CHAPTER IV

PREVIEW TO INFERNO

IT was the week before D-Day in Southern France, and at various Mediterranean points I saw men, boats and equipment on their way to the French Riviera; and the great armadas were awesome in their power and significance. Every one and everything was ready, almost every one was silent—and there is no silence so deep as war's silence! I watched demonstrations of dive-bombing with General John K. Cannon, whose men call him "Uncle Joe," although he is no relative of the famous Congressman. I stood with him as planes dove at a speed of more than five hundred miles an hour. The miscalculation of even one-half a second meant missing the target by many yards, but the dive-bombers were so numerous and the bombs so many and so powerful that lakes of fire smothered whole areas. Flames burst and blazed, both on earth and water. It might have been a preview of Dante's Inferno!

I visited parachute troops and airborne soldiers, many of whom had been in earlier campaigns. Some were entering combat for the first time. I felt for them what they did not feel for themselves, for to them their own heroism is commonplace. One decorated paratrooper, not yet twenty, deprecated his own bravery to pay tribute to others. "Probably the only reason I got a cross," he said, "was because I happened to be noticed. To me the chaps who deserve medals are the chaplains who search out the wounded in the front lines and stay with them until help comes. They don't have to, but they know there is

39

nothing more terrifying than lying alone, lost and helpless. And I know it too!"

I attended the briefings of some of the air missions that preceded the landings. With prayers I watched many take-offs, and thankfully I sometimes saw the return of all the planes. I saw photographs of places and defenses both before and after the bombs had fallen. These pictures show even the pickets placed upright in all level areas where landings of airborne troops might be attempted, for the posts cast shadows on the ground. Everything is shown in the greatest detail—except death.

I had planned to say Mass for a group of soldiers who were to take part in the invasion. It was raining and many of the boys had driven miles in open trucks in the downpour. Suddenly three more trucks drove up and several hundred sailors piled out and gathered with us around the altar built in a grove. As these men knelt in the mud and rain, I noticed the names stencilled on their sailors' slickers and realized the great number of nationalities represented in our country, united to form America's body and soul. Men from every State in the Union were there, men whose forebears had come from every region in the world, and they were kneeling before the altar of Him whom they acknowledged as the Commander-in-Chief of their souls. It was a gathering of humble men, and my heart was stirred with the emotional strain of giving Communion to boys, overflowing and ripe with life, some of whom, I knew, would die before the day would end. When I told them of my admiration for them, and thanked them for this expression of their faith, one soldier said, simply, typically and truly, "A fella *has* to have deep faith, Father, to come so far and stay so long in this weather!"

Another youngster, a lean, red-headed, friendly sailor, asked me if I would write a postscript to a letter he had just written home. I wanted to, of course, but it was impossible to do so without the rain blotting out each word as I wrote it, so the lad suggested that we go under the tailboard of a truck. And we did. This boy told me that he, and a number of the other sailors with him, had seen service together in the Pacific, and the letter he asked me to read and mail was an expression, he said, of what all the boys aboard his troopship felt about their chaplain. And because that letter conveyed to his own loved ones at home what is in the hearts and minds of thousands of boys in every part of the world today, I felt others should have the privilege of sharing that letter with me. He said I might make a copy:

"Dear Mom and Dad:

"First-off I want to tell you something I know will make you happy. It's not only about me . . . it's about the boys I'm with and also about one of the swellest fellows I ever met . . . our ship's chaplain. He lives our life and talks our language! We go to him with all our troubles and we even beef to him about the chow . . . and he listens. His cathedral is in a corner of the mess, and its stained-glass windows are portholes, small and round, stained only with salt water. We ourselves built for him the table he uses for an altar; and all that goes on the altar, and his vestments, are in a little black bag . . . and you'd be surprised maybe, and glad to know, how every one of us feels *safe* because of him and it. Everything else we have for the services exists only in our imagination, or in our memories. He never lectures or sermonizes. He just talks to us and his talks are always full of praise and encouragement. The sight of soldiers and sailors at prayer, any place, any time, he once said, is something to remember. But it is truly an inspiration to see hard-fisted, hard-fighting, hard-headed but not hard-hearted sailors kneeling in devotion aboard ship just before going into action.

"Whenever we feel scarey or know there's a big show coming off, there's a long line of us waiting outside his quarters; and some are not Catholics. He gives us all his blessing and advice; and when there's an emergency alarm, he gives general absolution. God alone knows what this man has done for us and means to us. And while none of us *wants* to die, Mom, this man makes the fighting and dying easier. I'm sure he's the only man aboard ship who doesn't long to go home, and one day when I asked him *why* he answered: 'For me home is where God's work is, and for me, God's work is here.'

"He can be funny too. He had little blue cards printed which he called ration tickets, which say no one is allowed more than five minutes' crying or beefing time in any twenty-four hours!

"Father doesn't always stay on the ship. When we stormed a beachhead he was right with us. I've seen him minister to the wounded and dying, knee-deep in the jungle mud, with rain pouring down his face, his clothes drenched; and some of my buddies went to confession and received Communion from him in their fox-holes!

"No one *can* take your place with me, but, if anyone could, he is the one, for he is mother, father and friend to us all. Yet, if he knew that I was writing about him and praising him this way, I'm afraid I'd lose him as a friend, for he keeps our secrets and expects us to keep his."

To me, this letter is a testament of man's faith in man, inspired by his faith in God and service to his country; and the vastness of that service struck me as I flew over our invasion fleets! The air-sight of these ships, covering great squares of miles, is unforgettable. Protecting warships, cruisers and destroyers were on all sides of the ships carrying troops and supplies. Airplanes zoomed before, above and all around the great flotillas. Every one who was to take part in the invasion, every one who knew anything about it, was tense, yet breathed a spirit of confidence in success, and nurtured well-founded hopes that our losses would not be severe. But, I reflected, there *would* be losses, and they would be severe to those who sustained them.

I wished to go with the troops who were to land on the first day of the invasion, and just missed the opportunity, but I did go to France a few days after the first landings, and thus was able to see more people and visit more places than if I had gone on D-Day. I had the choice of flying or of accompanying troops on a landing ship. I wanted to go both ways, but the time element was important and I chose the two-hour air route in preference to the two-day boat-ride. Among my fellow passengers in the plane were General Daniel Noce and Ambassador Robert Murphy, who were going to France on a mission.

It was an indescribable moment, when we first saw the coast of France. We reached it at Cap d'Antibes and flew westward along the coast of the Riviera over the isles of St. Margaret and St. Honoré. At Cannes, we flew very close to the shore line, and about a mile above it. American warships were bombarding, and we could see the flashes of flame and bursts of smoke from the ships, and also the pall where the missiles fell. Cannes itself was still occupied by the Germans. We flew south and southwestward, following the coast for many miles, and landed on the first airstrip that the Allies had bulldozed out of French soil in this invasion. It was just being completed and was heavy

with dust from the bulldozers that were still working on it from
planes landing and leaving. We went by jeep into the interior
of France on our way to meet General Alexander M. Patch,
commander of the Seventh Army, whose headquarters were
about sixty miles away. From our landing places near St. Tropez
we drove to the shore at Cavalaire, an Allied landing beach still
teeming with craft and alive with invading troops. Prayerfully
I watched numberless "cornucopias" of Americans poured into
France to shed their blood in pledge to her and to us; and I
wished that their valor, strength and selfless spirit could girdle
the earth and be reflected in the hearts and minds of all at home
to sustain and inspire them.

Following the beautiful Corniche Drive threading between
mountain and sea, we cut into the interior between Toulon
and Hyères, and arrived at headquarters only to learn that the
General was in the field. So, on we drove for another thirty
miles and found General Patch conferring with General Lucian
K. Truscott at his corps headquarters. We were near the town
of Rians, and here I said my first Mass on French soil. The
altar, built by the boys themselves, was set up under a clump
of trees in an open field, and mingling with our American soldiers were many French peasants from the neighboring countryside, forming a deep semicircle around the homemade altar.
This is a part of France which few Americans have visited, even
in peacetime, and these Frenchmen were tearfully happy as
Ambassador Murphy and I spoke to them in their own language.
As we rode along, we were everywhere greeted with joy and
enthusiasm; and judging by the warmth of their reception, I
think General Patch and Mr. Murphy could be elected to office
in many liberated towns and cities, if the democratic processes
of government were in operation! However, the American policy

and desire is to help the French people re-establish themselves, and then to leave France to the French.

General Patch flew back to headquarters in his Cub plane, a plane so small that it can take off and land almost anywhere; and we returned by jeep. During my days in Southern France, I was a guest of the General, who had just been nominated a Lieutenant General by President Roosevelt. Tall, thin, baldish, with light-blue eyes and characteristic deep parenthetical wrinkles on his face, he is a rhythmic, tireless human dynamo. The picture of him is deeply engraved in my memory. I sat with him one evening, as he listened to a broadcast about his achievements and the achievements of his Seventh Army— a man utterly thoughtless of himself, the hero of Guadalcanal, and now the heroic spirit of the Seventh Army. Always in closest personal contact with his officers and men, the General gets places, not only in his Cub plane and jeep but with his own rangy strides. He gets things done by example, by direction, and I think also by "jet-propulsion"! Once he said to me: "We have violated all the rules in the book of war, but in the circumstances it was the right thing to do."

By his startling, stunning tactics, General Patch breached some coast defenses and others he cut off and surrounded. Fanning out his forces, his men plunged ahead in all directions, save to the southward, for the word "retreat" had been cancelled out of American Army dictionaries! He inspired every officer and man, regardless of fatigue or shortage in food and equipment, to continue the advance with maximum energy and endurance, so that the day of victory might be speeded. One of the chaplains whom I met in Southern France told me an interesting story about the advance. It was so rapid that in new bivouac areas the bodies of dead German soldiers were frequently found, and Father Jordan Brown found two on the spot he picked to pitch his tent. He was ready to bury the two bodies, and taking hold of them, was startled to find them actually alive and armed! He commanded them to get up and walk ahead of him, and he delivered them to a Major and they became prisoners of war! However, my admiration for Father Brown's initiative and courage was a bit dampened when I heard the story of some Germans who wished to surrender to an American officer so tired that he said: "Please come back tomorrow to surrender!"

Unfortunately, the stories tinged with humor are far outnumbered by those tainted with tragedy. From many persons I heard almost unbelievable stories of Nazi atrocities. The Germans forbade chaplains to administer to innocent people condemned to death as hostages, and one French priest was shot by the Nazis when he attempted to aid one of the wounded German soldiers. One night the Gestapo entered a monastery, ordered the priests to assemble, accused them of having concealed arms, and demanded to know where they were hidden. When no one replied, the officer ordered five of the eighty-five priests to be shot and all of the eighty-five stepped forward! He then picked five of his own choosing, who were tortured and afterwards executed by machine gun in the presence of their companions. If the hearts and brains of men were not crazed by war, human beings could not be so inhumane as to inflict upon their fellowmen the savage, violent atrocities conceived and perpetrated by the Nazis. Human hatreds have become seething, swirling currents of passion, threatening to sweep away every vestige of humanity; and only when the tides of passion turn from lust, greed and hatred into equally strong passions for good can men live in harmony, security and peace.

In contrast, there is one almost unbelievable story that I *want* to believe. An American soldier told me: "I saw twenty Nazis pray! During a service near Aix I counted twenty Germans kneeling in prayer alongside my buddies, and it was good to see that there are some Germans who believe there is a greater ruler than Hitler and a greater power than Naziism."

It was in St. Maximin, where I had stopped at the famous shrine of Mary Magdalene, that the mother, father and wife of an imprisoned Frenchman came to see me. The father, a veteran of the last war, and the mother were bowed with age, but they were bowed with grief also, and grief too had aged the youthful wife. Tearfully they besought me to intercede with the Allied authorities to save their son and husband, who that morning had been arrested as a collaborationist. I realized both my incompetency to judge, and my powerlessness to intervene. But I did recommend them to some one I knew, and asked him to listen to their story to see whether something should and could be done. But in the heat of war it is extremely and tragically difficult to get accurate knowledge concerning individual cases. Causes are more important than lives; and in war's economy the life of one man weighs but little. These people were weeping because their son and husband would, they thought, be sentenced to ten or fifteen years in prison. What happened to that man I had no way of finding out, but I came to realize that the prevailing circumstances tend to dispense with prison sentences, for earlier that very morning I had seen the bodies of four Frenchmen lying side by side on the road! One was very young; all were shoeless but otherwise fully clothed; and all had been shot! They may have been killed by Germans as spies, or by Frenchmen as collaborationists; they may have been patriots or traitors.

War had plunged me into the midst of human nature in the rough and in the raw, and the other horn of almost every dilemma seemed to be death. I spent one day near Toulon, then in German hands and strongly defended. German shells shook the altar and shook me as I was saying Mass in a French home that had been requisitioned by the military. A French priest, who had lost a leg in the service, had turned a dining-room table into an altar, and opened the French doors that led onto a piazza so that the soldiers actually manning batteries around the house and in the garden could hear the service. About a dozen French soldiers were on the piazza, and other groups, soldiers and civilians, were in the garden. Added to the noise of cannon and machine-gun fire was the volley that ended the lives of two French "collaborationists." After that experience, I needed something to eat and I was glad and grateful to the French priest for my breakfast of sour wine and hard salami.

Among war's most pitiful scourges are the hatreds bred among peoples of the same nations. War turns heads and twists hearts, making patriots traitors and traitors patriots. One man, who had known many Germans before the war and had continued his association with a German officer in occupied France, said he maintained his contact with the enemy for the welfare of his fellow countrymen. It was substantiated that he had saved several of them from execution, and had had others liberated from prison. Today he himself is in prison as a collaborationist, but he hopes that when he is brought to trial the court will be convinced that he was loyal to his country.

War also hardens hearts. I talked with a young French girl who had spent four years in America, making her living as a salesgirl in a New York department store. She was intensely patriotic and had returned to France to drive an ambulance in the Medical Corps of the French Army. We discussed France, her internal problems, "collaboration," and "purification," still another name for "epuration," which eliminates collaborationists as well as Nazis. I told her the story of the old parents whose son had been jailed. I expected that she would feel as badly as I. But I was mistaken. "He should have thought of his mother, father and wife before he collaborated," she said. I took time to explain that denunciations and recriminations, which are floating freely about the whole world, are not final proofs of guilt. I told her that I still believed accusations were not convictions and that every one was entitled to a fair trial before punishment, especially if the punishment be death.

Every Frenchman and every well-wisher of France hopes that the liberation of France will be her resurrection and will re-establish her greatness. But the realization of this hope and prayer is a longer and more involved process than the march up the Rhone Valley and down the Loire, the Seine and the Somme to the Swiss border and on to Berlin. Liberation must mean more than the defeat and expulsion of the Germans. It must mean salvation, regeneration and peace. And to us Americans liberation must mean more than the destruction of French towns and the killing of French people, even if in driving the enemy from their strongholds our advancing armies have been obliged to damage homes and churches. It was ever our wish to destroy the wolves, and not the flock. And it was with sorrow we were forced to demolish cities and towns—not as heartless destroyers but as fearless liberators.

For miles and miles we drove through peaceful countryside. Excellent roads there were, shaded by sycamores, maples and poplars. Great groves of pine and cork trees covered the hillsides and valleys; and, as the saying goes, "with the cork and the vineyards in this region the people produce everything except the bottles." We covered considerable territory in plane and jeep, and even in a sedan, for the Germans had not had time to damage the roads. They had, however, placed pikes in apparently every field in South France to obstruct an airborne invasion.

In some parts of France it was hard to realize there was a war until suddenly a shattered, shell-scarred village loomed before us. And one of the most gruesome scenes was a cemetery with its monuments and its graves burst open from a recent bombing. It was a dead town, with its buried and unburied dead. I talked with a solitary Frenchman outside the spattered ruins of his home. He represented the immortal spirit that can help to give back to France unity and life. I asked whether it was a German or an American bombardment that had destroyed his home, and he answered, "Not the Germans, not the Americans; War destroyed it! But I am going to rebuild it." War is the world's enemy and we are still waging war to destroy War.

On this trip I got close to war and closer than ever I should be. One man with me said, "We are avoiding danger, going towards it!" War's awful, grimy, gory side was everywhere evident. With all the modern means of war, man is magnificently successful in destroying man! I saw paratroops and other airborne troops who had been shot as they plunged down through the sky, and crashed or were crushed against the great pointed stakes that had been planted in every level spot. I saw shrapnel-gouged and torn infantry soldiers. All the tragedy of war, all the pathos of human suffering, all the glory of victory, human and divine, are fashioned from our boys' purest sacrifices and from their blood. Sad, starved, unsatisfied faces stunned my brain and wrung my heart. Not poverty, not sickness, were to me the most horrible things to behold, but the crass, craven cruelty of man's inhumanity to man. One soldier, who looked like a schoolboy lying on his litter, whispered to me, "I know I am dying, Father, and my only sorrow is for my mother. Tell her, please, I offered my life to my country and to God, and He has chosen to accept it. I have no bequest to leave her except the assurance of my faithfulness to duty." This boy held no inquest on the past. His own life ending, he did not revile or blame any one. He did not envy those who were to live longer, and his selflessness is a challenge to all who would dare corrupt that bequest with anything less than a just and lasting peace!

I saw truck-loads of German prisoners roll by. Most of the prisoners were young, so young that at the war's outbreak they could not have known what the war was about—and they never will know! Some looked surly, bold and defiant, but most of them were subdued and bewildered, the product of Nazi education and now its dregs.

All along the Mediterranean, from the Gulf of St. Tropez to within three miles of Toulon, and into the interior as far as Aix I went, and all the time and everywhere there was stark contrast between the peace of nature and the war of human beings. Vineyards and melon patches were alongside, and sometimes topside, of mine fields. The blue hills along the Mediterranean foregrounded the higher peaks of the Maritime Alps. All nature was peaceful, and yet from nature's bosom spouted booming, barking, screeching death, as relentlessly we pressed the enemy and advanced. We seemed very close to a complete military triumph. One day, when I was with General Mike O'Daniel, he described the campaign, its results, its progress and its objectives. He swept his hands over the region that only that day had come into Allied possession. And as his fingers pronged the map, so the armies of the Allies were pronging the land, seeking to touch fingers with American and French Armies from the north, to clasp them over the heart of France and squeeze the enemy from her land.

During my days in France I saw also some of the "fodder" of victory. All that I have read in the Bible describing war or death did not make on me the grotesque impression made by dead German soldiers as I saw them matted together in great masses awaiting burial. Some of the Germans had been killed only that day. Others had been longer dead. They had obeyed Hitler's orders to take root in the ground! The smell was indescribably terrible and the sight was indescribably awful. The country people were burying the decomposing bodies under the supervision and with the aid of men and boys of the French Forces of the Interior, who wore civilian clothes with distinctive F.F.I. armbands. They had cloths over their mouths and noses, but it was impossible, I am sure, to filter the stench from the air. From wheelbarrows and from carts, bodies and parts of bodies were dumped into great holes. Sometimes bodies were fused together in a solid, shapeless lump of clay. One German soldier seemed to me, for some inexplicable reason, to resemble the traditional figure of Mars. He was sprawled in the mud, his left hand under his sunken, battered head, his right hand grasping his blood-stained canteen, and blood, too, drooled from his mouth. Death was pouring more blood into the chalice for Mars, already drunk, to drink!

I thought of our own dead, wounded and missing. I thought of our cemeteries and hospitals; and I thought of our homes. I thought of bombs falling on London, Warsaw, Rotterdam, Antwerp, Belgrade, Coventry, and on a thousand other places.

I thought of bombs on Milan and Berlin. And I thought of what bombs could do to New York, Chicago, and all America. What has happened to civilization? Can humanity save itself? Can something peaceful grow from this fertilization by the cannon fodder of the youth of all nations? Can we weave a strong, unbreakable peace from the weak, broken threads hanging from the fabric of war? Our leaders, and we ourselves, face the challenge of all the dead. And as I drove in silence through lanes of dusty rhododendrons, along the Mediterranean on my way to board a plane for England, I prayed God that we, the living, may meet that challenge, and that the souls of the heroic dead may have eternal rest from the hell they found on earth.

CHAPTER V

IN MUTUAL DEVOTION

D ARKNESS was melting into daylight as I landed at an English airport and saw a Flying Fortress, mortally wounded, come limping back from a mission. I had flown through the flaming skies of France, over her land teeming with men and clanging with arms, over her cemeteries with their armies bivouacked in silence, straight into the face of sudden death! Again I was witness to the flame-like selfless heroism of those who daily die that we may live. Sprawling rag-doll figures of men parachuted from the plunging stricken plane as, fear-frozen, we awaited the inevitable plummet into the houses in its path. But just before the crash, almost like a human making a superhuman effort, the plane heaved upwards, just missed the houses, and then crashed to earth in the open field! The superhuman effort had spared homes and lives, but had cost the life of the pilot. Every day, I reflected, is truly a day of "wrath, wasting and misery," with the heavens and earth shaken and the world being tried by fire.

General Eisenhower had kindly sent an aide to meet me and he, too, was at the airport when the plane crashed. The co-pilot, the last man to parachute from the plane, told us the pilot had ordered the crew to bail out and that he thought the pilot himself would follow them. Instead, he had stayed with his plane, apparently hoping to guide it to safety. Sadly and silently we stood, grieved at the loss of a life, inspired by the way it was given.

Driving drearily along the road toward London on our way to the American Embassy, the Colonel broke into our silence, saying that he would immediately recommend the pilot for a military award. While I realize that awards for valor are the only tangible tokens that our nation can give to our heroes, I know that our real appreciation and deepest gratitude can be revealed only in our own determination to be worthy of their martyrdom. Terrifying testimony to the martyrdom of others in this fantastic, modern, merciless warfare was the sight of the giant gashes that had been bitten out of London by fiendish robots. In many places I have seen the devastation caused by bombings and the demolition of entire cities, but seeing the damage that a single robot can cause was to me appalling and ominous, and I was awed at the power of science applied to destruction. The fundamental purpose of science is the progression of the human race, but today, tragically and with frightening contradiction, the advancement of science seems to parallel the retrogression of civilization. We have made of science a Pandora's Box. Of this story there are two contradictory versions: one, that the box was filled with blessings; the other, that it was filled with miseries. War is the key that has released its miseries; peace is the only key to its blessings.

When I called on Ambassador Winant I was fortunate enough to meet at the same time General Spaatz, General "Wild Bill" Donovan and General Anderson. They had just arrived from Italy after a very-high-altitude flight of a few hours over German-held territory. It was a real reunion, for I had not seen the Ambassador or General Spaatz since my last trip to London and North Africa, though Bill had come to see me in New York just before I left for overseas. We talked "shop" and, all over the world, shop talk is war talk. Naturally, the Ambassador and the three Generals, all veterans of the first World War, engaged in professional talk about the war's progress, its cost and its significance. But one need not be a professional soldier to know that maps and statistics, however expressive they may be, do not show the complete mosaic of this crucified, blood-drunken world! The results of this war cannot be fully appraised by reading large-scale maps or large-scale figures. The rewards of victory cannot be measured by territory gained or in numbers of enemy killed or captured; nor can the cost of victory be evaluated by the lists of our own casualties. War is terribly human and inhumane, and a most terrible human affliction; for even a war waged in the cause of resisting unjust aggression has inevitably many grim consequences. War is infectious, contagious and contaminating, a plague of the mind, heart, body and soul. War rolls into a terrifying avalanche the resources of nature with the forces of human nature, plunging man down the mountainside of civilization!

It was nearly dusk when I left the Embassy, but I wanted to try to get to the general hospital at —— before nightfall. A General Hospital cares for at least fifteen hundred patients, and while it takes a full day to go from bed to bed, as I always do, there was still time to go through many of the wards and say a word to each patient, and with one young pilot I spent nearly an hour. Each soldier has a story and each soldier *is* a story! When I talk man to man with individual soldiers, the dangers, horrors and consequences of war are most deeply impressed upon me. The airman longed to talk alone with some one, to open his mind and heart, and I was grateful to be that "some one." As he talked freely of his home, his mother and himself, he painted for me not only his own life-picture, but a picture characteristic of our boys throughout the world.

The spring of this boy's ambition had been the joy that his

success would bring to his parents. Yet, even in the midst of his studies, though his "serial number" seemed far away, he could not shut the war from his mind. Conflicts between the duty which he owed to his country and the duty he owed to his mother and father disturbed and distressed him. He was eager to enlist, but he was the oldest of five children and wanted to share with his parents the responsibility for them. Finally, he knew there was no conflict. He realized that his duty to himself, his family, and his country were one—to become a soldier. He could think of no way to break the news to his mother, so he enlisted, went home to her in his uniform and found that *she* was the real hero! She said that she was proud of him, and she praised him.

Despite his own determination and his mother's bravery, home-leaving was unbelievably hard. Thinking of her, he became sick at heart, and homesickness left no room for any other feeling. He tried to forget home, but it took two months before "indoctrination" enabled him to acquire enough "forgetting" to have what the army called the "proper mental status." Transferred to a replacement center, he was taught to load a plane with bombs and to arm it with machine guns. When an officer asked if there was any special branch of the service he preferred, he said he would like to be a pilot. His request was promptly refused with the comment that "in the Army every man is as important as any other," and he was trained to be an aerial gunner! He realized how close he was to actual war when his best friend was killed in a plane crash. It might have happened to him, he thought. He pictured his parents receiving the news of his death, and he was frightened! As this boy talked, I knew he was reliving, as I was living with him, those first few months in the service.

Granted ten days' leave, he flew home. The days passed as

in a dream, and before he realized it his furlough was over, and his mother and father were at the airport to see him off. It was midnight. Just as he was entering the plane he heard his mother scream his name. He turned for one last look, but she was standing in front of a spotlight and the glare blinded him so that he could not see her. Fearful questions tumbled through his mind. Would he ever see her again? Would he be killed? Would she die before he returned? In the darkness of the plane he tried to sleep, and fitfully, he passed the night.

Hesitating, he said: "Father, I have no right to burden you with my troubles—yet I have been lonely—terribly lonely—and a fellow needs to talk to some one or he'll go mad. Over here, even in groups, each one of us is still terribly alone!" I told him I was glad to listen, and he smiled his gratitude, and continued.

A few more weeks of training and he was aboard ship crossing the Atlantic. The voyage lasted two weeks and, after that confinement, he felt that anything would be a relief. Three weeks' intensive training in England and he and his crew were ready for combat; ready to carry bombs to drop on German cities and to fight off enemy planes. "And I had been taught," he said, "to love and respect my neighbor as myself!"

On the morning of his first mission he was nervous. There were so many things to do that only once did he think of home and that was during the ride from the briefing room to the plane. He thought of home, and prayed.

There was little flak over the target and not much trouble from enemy fighters. On that trip, the city was too close to our own fighter bases in England for the Germans to dare much resistance. But on the next raid, the first attempt of the Americans to bomb a great German city, it was rough aplenty.

"Long before we got to the city," he said, "the Luftwaffe was up there to meet us. Planes plunged into the sea and to the ground. Some were German and some were ours. There were ten men in each American plane, but only one in each German plane! We had expected the Germans to let us go alone over the target, so that their planes would not be hit by their own heavy flak. But the Germans had other ideas and were out to get us, slashing fiercely at our formation despite the flak danger to themselves. Our tail gunner kept reporting, 'Another B-17 just blew up,' and he said it so calmly that I began to dislike him for it. After all, I thought, each plane meant ten lives and ten lives meant ten telegrams!

"When we returned to our base, I tried to be matter-of-fact and cool, like the boys who had been on many missions. Every one tries, and this helps every one else. Two days after this mission, I was awakened at three-thirty in the morning. Briefing was an hour later. The briefing room was more crowded than usual, and I sensed that something extraordinary was up. It was a priority target, the Intelligence Officer announced, and vital to Germany's industry. He gave us the data of time and place for the rendezvous, and forecast the weather. Fighters and flak would be rough, he said, for we were to penetrate deeply into Germany, and he read a letter from the General telling us how important it was that this target be thoroughly blasted. After the briefing, many of the boys went to the Chaplain and received Communion.

"We put on our heavy clothes and trucked out to the plane. Shortly, we were airborne. We fought our way to the target, bombed through heavy flak and began the return. Fighters kept diving through our formation, shooting, being shot at and shot down. Many of ours were hit, and some fell or fluttered earthwards. Our plane was knocked out of formation, and the Germans came in for the kill! We fought back, knocked down five, and I was hit. My head spun round, and I fell. My throat was dry and I tasted blood. I was to be the first one of the crew to go, I thought, as I lay waiting to lose consciousness. But I was not afraid to die, I told myself, for I was trading my life for a clear conscience!

"I woke up in bed. My wound is not serious, and soon I shall be flying again, but I find myself looking for the end of the war and once more analyzing myself. I have given much to the war and, unashamedly, I admit that I am one of the soldiers who is fighting to get home; and home is the only thing that I want out of the war. I know the war has changed me, but home just *must* be the same. That's my story. I wanted you to hear it, and I wanted you to know that my war aim is home, and my peace-aim is to stay there."

Our soldiers have been criticized for saying they are fighting to get home. Why should they be? We went to war to save our homes, and it is to keep them secure, and to restore others to their homes, that we are still at war. As for home being the same, could I tell him that not only are many homes different, but that many people are indifferent? Could I tell him about the veteran lieutenant, only twenty-four, returned to New York after twenty-three months' combat service, who came to see me, and asked, "What's the matter with every one, or is the trouble with me? I longed to get home, and now I want to get back. I feel more at home in war than I feel here." He knew his family were proud of him, and grateful for his safe return. He had prayed that home would be the same, but finding it the same, felt himself strangely resentful, because he sensed that the cost of this war had not penetrated the hearts of those it had not struck. Indoctrination to war had not shocked him as rudely as did return from war! Yet, it would have been useless, and perhaps wrong, for me to have disillusioned this boy, for when he does return he may not feel as did the lieutenant, since all minds and hearts do not react identically to the bewildering contradictions that torment war's men.

Just as I was leaving the hospital, I met a Chaplain I knew, and he invited me to stay the night with him. The day had been long and I was physically tired and emotionally tried. I gladly accepted his invitation, and went with him to his quarters in the hospital. Tired as I was, I did not go to bed, because the Chaplain wanted to talk to some one, and again I was grateful to be that "someone."

Several months ago, after two years' service in the South Pacific, he had been assigned to this base hospital. When first he landed at —— in the Pacific, he found an abandoned chapel nestling on a muddy hillside. In a few short months it was transformed into a church, with rugs, drapes and statues, and with Mary, guardian in the sanctuary, watching the whole night long. The boys came in by day and night to talk to her and to her Son in His tabernacle. They made Him the center of their lives and told Him their joys, fears, hopes and sorrows. Every morning at six o'clock, He would find at least fifty boys kneeling and praying for strength when the going was hard; and before Him boys and girls joined hands and hearts in marriage, and boys knelt as the Chaplain pinned their first bars on their shoulders.

The time came when they had to leave their little church, and the Chaplain went with the troops into the field and jungle. Then, for an altar, they usually had a folding table, and for their church a grassy or muddy slope, but on that crude altar the Lord came down just the same, to be cradled in the Chaplain's trembling fingers and to nourish and strengthen the souls of his men. "Life in the Army has not changed me much," the padre said, "except in one very important detail—I think I'm a better priest than I was."

No one could witness the devotion of these lads without becoming better. If only their loved ones could kneel in a chapel at twilight and watch them as they tell their beads, or tread wearily the way of the cross! If only they could see their boys as I daily have seen them in the greatest picture of this world's worst war, kneeling in prayer, earnestly asking His guidance and protection! In mud and sand, in heat and cold, in sleet and rain, in many lands, on many battle fronts, I have seen this precious picture of our boys reflected in the cup of my chalice, and I long to print this picture on the hearts and memories of those at home as it is imprinted on mine. Then would they drain themselves of selfishness and bigotry, and emulate our boys in selfless devotion to God and country, so to be worthy of that reflection and of the blood that soaks the earth from end to end!

I should have gone to bed, but the Chaplain kept me up talking to me about his experiences, some inspiring, some gruesome, some humorous. He told me the story of several nuns who had been evacuated from Japanese-held territory to the army hospital in Guadalcanal while he was stationed there. When they climbed out of the dusty reconnaissance car, their white faces were sad, pinched and worn, and their white robes were streaked and stained black with dirt and dust. The youngest nun carried a tattered canvas bag containing all they possessed in the world, all they were able to take with them in their crazy-quilt flight through the jungle and across the Coral Sea.

At first they were shy, confused and a bit frightened; but

their bewilderment and sadness melted as they saw signs of a civilization they had left behind more than twenty years ago to devote themselves to the care of the lepers in New Ireland. Comfortable and care-free for a few fleeting days, they slept in clean white beds in neat, insect-free rooms; listened to the radio and, best of all, after having lived for many months on a little rice and water, they now had fresh, plentiful food. To the surprise of the army nurses, the oldest nun had never heard a radio; but the greatest novelty, to the nuns themselves, was a washing-machine—which they immediately learned to use, like children with a new toy. When they left the hospital, their garments were once again white, starched and clean—renewed and refreshed—as were their spirits.

"One day you laugh and joke with a lad and the next you lay him to rest," the Chaplain said, recalling the Sunday he saw a Jap air-bomb make a direct hit on a jeep carrying three American soldiers. They never knew what hit them. He picked up parts of the men within a radius of three hundred yards from the spot, and the biggest fragments were two right hands and one left. He had to fingerprint them six times, each hand! One soldier, unnerved by the sight of watching him, said as he tagged the last hand, "Boy, you're hard," and when the Chaplain looked up and the boy saw the tears running down his cheeks, he put his hand on the Padre's shoulder and said, "Gee, I'm sorry, Sir."

Burying our boys is one of the hardest, saddest tasks of the war, and often one of the most dangerous. The Padre told me about Captain Fred Andrews of Galveston, Texas, a Protestant Chaplain atttached to an Infantry battalion. Sympathetic, understanding, unfailing in his devotion, he was invaluable to officers, men and other Chaplains. In war, the strong bolster the spiritually as well as the physically weak, and Chaplain Andrews was a constant comfort to all men whose souls were troubled. When he was awarded the Silver Star each man of his outfit was prouder than he, who in his natural humility felt no pride except in his service to God and man. Tireless, he conducted, often after midnight, burial services for his boys, so that no one entrusted to his care was laid to rest without his ministrations.

Chaplains and their boys share a deep-rooted mutual devotion, and while Chaplains take great risks to serve their boys, the boys also risk their lives to help one another. I know that, in every theatre of war, last Christmas, hundreds of Catholic soldiers were enabled to attend midnight Mass because hundreds of their non-Catholic comrades "did the turn" for them in combat! Our boys are brave and courageous, yet childlike, confiding and lavishly generous. I have seen cigarettes, candies, coins for the needy, all tumble out of their pockets, just as did marbles not so long ago when they still sat in their schoolrooms, and only the other day I learned from a Frenchman that an American Unit, comprised of boys of every religious faith, had presented him with five thousand dollars to help repair a Catholic church that their own bombs had damaged.

In war, spiritual as well as military objectives are necessary, and while there are always scoffers, some who come to scoff remain to pray! One blustering paratrooper said to me: "Whoever said there are no atheists in foxholes is crazy." Another, overhearing him, answered: "It's easy to see you're not a veteran! Prayer is the first thing we think of when we're cornered. It is as instinctive as eating." The next evening I was surprised and happy when that paratrooper joined us in our sunset service for those of his battalion who had lost their lives.

For a respite from sorrow and tragedy, I told the Chaplain

of an incident that occurred in Sicily. It was the time when mules were being shot because they blocked the road and interfered with the progress of our tanks. Thus, to save the life of a mule and at the same time to further the war effort, a Chaplain became the owner of a mule! Wet and cold, living on K-rations for many days, not only were the spirits of his men bogged down, but they themselves were bogged down in the mud and their advance was halted. The Chaplain led his mule to a neighboring monastery and, leaving the mule and a supplement of kind words with the Prior of the Monastery, he returned to his outfit leading a cow, and the steaks were a rare and delicious treat for his soldiers!

The black mist-heavy night was well on towards morning when I finally fell asleep, but I realized the truth of what the young airman had said—if you don't talk to someone, you'll go mad—and I hoped that I had helped both Chaplain and airman, for both of them had helped me.

On the fifth anniversary of the violation of Poland, I attended Mass for Poland's martyred dead. Archbishop Griffin of Westminster presided at the Mass in the Brompton Oratory, the church that Cardinal Newman had founded through the generosity of the Duke of Norfolk, and which the Cardinal had made the center of Catholicism in London years before Westminster Cathedral was built. Out of love and sorrow for Poland, thousands attended the ceremony, pledging their abiding faith in her resurrection. The oratory has been the scene of national rejoicings and mournings for hundreds of occasions, but I do not believe any could have been more poignant than the occasion of this prayer for Poland. It recalled to me the day, five years before, when German hordes had burst into Poland, overpowering and blighting her. That day I had offered Mass in St. Patrick's Cathedral, thronged with thousands of sobbing people. Then I had said that Poland would rise again—that Poland *must* rise again or Europe would fall. And the commemoration in London, these five years later, bore witness to that truth, for those who think they are burying Poland are but planting the seeds of another war!

President Raczkiewicz, tall and somber, occupied a place in the sanctuary. After the services, I went with him to luncheon at the Polish Embassy. Heart-rending as it is for me to condole with the father of a family bereft of his children, it was even sadder to commiserate with the head of a nation grieved by the desecration of his country and the slaughter of her sons. What happens to Poland will be prophetic and set the pattern for what will happen to other valiant but small and helpless nations, for the fate of Poland is the barometer which will prove whether or not in our time the principles of the Atlantic Charter are to take root and bear fruit.

In 1939, Poland spurned "security" under German protection. She knew that Anglo-French help could not save her, yet she refused to accept the German terms, and suffered disaster. Poland's noble defiance of Germany has saved Europe and the world from the triumph of Naziism, and the price has been paid with the blood of her people and with her ravished land. Poland sees no essential difference between the German proposal she rejected five years ago and the offer of peace with security that Russia offers today. Sympathy and admiration are but a poor response to Poland's suffering and bravery. Poland must be a free, independent and sovereign nation if the Atlantic Charter is to be a living, meaningful document.

"The honor, the pride and cherished treasure of every English heart will be ruthlessly flung on the scrap-heap if Poland is not free," said Archbishop MacDonald of Edinburgh. And, he asked: "Why is it that the glorious manhood of our country has been sacrificed? Why is it that the flower of our youth has poured out its heart's blood on the battlefield? Why is it that we experienced God's intervention on the beaches of Dunkirk and in the Battle of Britain? We may conceal the truth from ourselves today, we may camouflage the facts and comfort ourselves with deceitful, soft-sounding words now, but one thing is certain: those guilty of the crime of liquidating Poland, if it comes to pass, will be scorned and despised by future generations; they will justly be regarded with horror for all time, as seared with the brand of Cain in the murder of a faithful ally and brother-nation in arms."

Poland has been loyal to herself, to her neighbors and to her Allies, and long the Poles have sung, "For our liberty and for yours." Will she now be erased from the book of life? Poland may be murdered, but she will never commit suicide!

That evening, Brendan Bracken, British Minister of Information, called for me and took me to supper at the Kemsleys'. Lord Kemsley is the publisher of a chain of newspapers and is close to the war, not only as a newspaperman, but also because he has six sons in military service, one of whom has been lost in action. Another boy, who was home on furlough, and Lady Kemsley were the only others at table. Lady Kemsley is a native of Mauritius, and since this island is so far distant and for the past few years has been almost inaccessible, she welcomed me just a bit more warmly, I thought, when I referred to her birthplace, which I had visited, as "The Pearl of the Indian Ocean"!

I was especially pleased to be the guest of the Kemsleys, because they gave me an accurate and intimate profile of England. They told me about General Sir Frederick Pile, the man on whom rested the responsibility of winning the latest Battle of Britain, the battle against the "buzz-bombs." Londoners were breathing more freely, now that the robot scourge was diminishing, but the scars from that scourge will long remain on the country and its people. General Pile commanded all the anti-aircraft forces of Britain, and it was he who built up the air-war defense to an almost impregnable strength. Men whom he trained, and methods which he adopted, have been responsible for the defensive measures used in Malta and throughout all the war areas. After five years of war, General Pile occupied the same position and command that he did at the war's beginning, and he was the only man of his rank with that honor. Brendan Bracken knew that I would enjoy meeting the General, and arranged for me to spend the entire next day with him, and I was with General "Tim," as he is called, on the day when the last V-1 robot plane hit England.

We met in mid-morning on a squally day and drove through the interminable stretches of South London, drab with war and gored by bombings, in livid and startling contrast to the lovely and historic country along the southern flank of the Thames Valley. The road led through quiet villages and past century-old homesteads, through woods of beech trees and open country dappled with silvery barrage-balloons off duty, sheltered in hollows from the boisterous wind. We saw the great House of Knole, once the home of Tudor Kings, and went on to Canterbury, down the southern escarpment, along the Pilgrim's Way. Driving along amid the chalk hills, through the orchards and hop gardens of the Kentish Weald, we reached the coast somewhere between Hastings and Rye. The Battle of Hastings, and its date 1066, are frequently the only bits of English historical erudition which Americans possess, and it was inevitable that I should mention that battle. But General Pile was more interested in the present battle.

The General, evidently, had never been a pessimist. He told me that even when Germany had overrun France, Belgium and Holland, and when, according to all the rules of logic, Britain had been beaten and England itself was about to be overrun by the Germans, still, quite illogically, he never believed this would, or could, happen. With reverent admiration he spoke of the pilots of the few Spitfire planes, whose engines were kept red-hot, and who seemed to be always in the sky against the Luftwaffe. Those pilots were the spirit of Britain and it was because of their courage that the Germans did not dare the invasion of England.

General Pile is a short, stocky, bronze-faced little dynamo of a man of sixty autumns. Like many of England's great Generals, he was born in Ireland. When admitted to Woolwich Military Academy, he stood seventy-seventh in a class of seventy-seven, but two years later in his final examinations he was thirty-sixth. General "Tim" served in South Africa, in India, and in France during the entire four years of the first World War. In the Army of Occupation he became a senior officer and, after that, promotions came rapidly. He became interested in mechanized warfare and, just before World War II, was made Commander-in-Chief of the Anti-Aircraft Command.

The General has chosen men of science for his Staff, for he believes that the importance of science in war cannot be exaggerated. Some of his Staff are professional soldiers, and others are professors who have become soldiers. Germany expected science to win the war for her, but instead science saved Britain from defeat. It was the British invention, radar, at that time secret, that helped Britain's pilots to give their comparatively small numbers the effectiveness of great fleets, so that each plane did the work of ten against the overwhelming number of enemy planes. General Pile patiently and simply explained radar, so that I might estimate its limitless uses. Radar, he said, was something absolutely new in war, and nothing else was completely new but merely an improvement in power, speed and maneuverability over what had been used in the last war.

Together with Britain's men, radar, location by radio, was the impregnable wall of defense that saved Britain. Radar was known to the Germans at the time of the Battle of Britain, but Germany, at that time, was not interested in its development for war, since it was considered to be useful primarily for defense purposes; and Germany was concerned only with the development of completely smothering offensive power. Defense was neither in her vocabulary nor in her mind. Britain, however, realizing her defensive needs, developed radar because she recognized its value as an effective method of detecting enemy aircraft. Radar can detect airplanes through clouds, and Britain's planes could remain on the ground until the moment of the approach of the enemy, and then the pilots knew exactly when and where to go to find them. Thus radar multiplied the effectiveness of pilots and planes. General Pile reminded me that radar was instrumental in winning not only the Battle of Britain but also the Battle of the Atlantic, for it located submarines and enabled the American and British Navies to destroy them.

The General explained each type of instrument, in great detail. I saw the men in action and the guns in operation, and, to give me an idea of the effectiveness of air defense against the "buzz-bombs," he told me that just two days before the Germans stopped discharging V-1's, one hundred and six bombs had been launched against London but only four of them had succeeded in getting through the barrage. I could not understand how it was possible for even one plane to get through that wall of gunfire forty thousand feet high, but before this defense was perfected, incalculable damage had been caused in this first battle in history against pilotless planes. In the ten-week-long battle, over nine thousand flying bombs were launched, and those that did get through destroyed or damaged a million houses and killed approximately nine thousand people. But the battle against the V-1 robot bombs was ending, for in addition to the practically impassable anti-aircraft defense provided by the shore batteries, there were airplanes constantly patrolling the Channel. These planes were charged with the double duty of informing those who manned the gun positions that robots had been launched, and of shooting them down, if possible, over the Channel before they reached the coast. On clear days, the General said, the robots could be spotted at great distances and once located either by radar, airplane or ground watch, everything else—elevation, speed, direction—was automatically computed, the proximate future position of the robot calculated and the fuse of the shell timed, so that definitely, accurately and inevitably shell and plane would meet, and every one of the latter brought down.

In addition to observing the operation of the radar equipment, I witnessed an impressive rocket barrage. The fuses of the rockets are adjusted so that the rockets burst in a complete cube of explosions. Some of the rockets carry strands of metal, and the airplane is either struck or entangled. Finally, in addition to the airplane patrols and the anti-aircraft guns and rockets, there is one more wall of defense: a balloon barrage which, while it is used principally for psychological reasons, to stop bombers piloted by humans, is also occasionally effective in intercepting the pilot-less robots. This balloon barrage justifies itself, said the General, even if it stops only one bomb.

The range of V-1 robot planes was about one hundred and fifty miles, and at a distance of one hundred miles they were launched with sufficient accuracy to fall within an area of approximately a four-by-five-mile quadrangle. Monitor gyro compasses held the robots on their course against cross winds and made compensation for drift, but headwinds impaired their accuracy.

General Pile generously praised American scientists, engineers, manufacturers and laboring men for developing and producing this radar equipment, the instrument of victory. He made no secret of the fact that if Germany had been able to use these flying bombs some months earlier, it would have made a vast difference in the progress of the war. A scourge of these bombs during the pre-invasion months could have horribly increased the loss of life and property and incalculably interfered with the war effort.

The Allied Intelligence had known, he said, that the robot bombs existed. They knew, too, the havoc they could spread throughout London, and that the life of every Londoner was in constant jeopardy, and preparations were made to combat them. The launching sites and the factories where the robots were being manufactured had been bombed, and anti-aircraft installations were made ready. But the most powerful and effective defense against the robots was radar. I saw dozens of places where robots had struck. Whole blocks had been obliterated and houses in the immediate area where they landed had been completely destroyed. Other houses in the vicinity had been denuded of shingles and clap-boards and left standing like skeletons. Death-dealing concussion swept over large areas, and on the bodies of some of the victims not even bruises were found. The explosive force of the bombs is horizontal. They make either no craters at all or very shallow ones. One bomb had fallen in a field of cabbages. There was no crater, and there were no cabbages—for every head had completely disappeared. General Pile told me that a bomb had exploded in a cow-pasture in Hatfield and when the cows that had survived were milked, the milk was sour! Another fantastic incident occurred when a bomb fell on a building, causing many deaths, though one man, asleep in his bed on the fifth floor, dropped the full five stories and was uninjured.

As we rode back to London, General Pile proudly told me of the bravery of the men who were responsible for the examination of the three robot bombs which had fallen as duds. It was necessary to examine them to find out how they were made and to learn all about them. The first engineer who volunteered to examine a robot brought with him a portable telephone in order to describe everything he did and everything he was going to do, so that if the robot blew up, the next man to attempt a similar task would know what to do and what to avoid doing. The first man to examine the first robot was killed as he was examining it; but, thanks to his heroism, and the information which he gave, the second man succeeded!

When we arrived back in London, we learned of the advance of the Allied troops into the Pas de Calais and the occupation of the bomb-launching area. The General said: "This Battle of Britain is nearly over. I hope I have shot myself out of a job. But," he added, "if we do not gain a lasting peace, you have witnessed the first battle of the next war."

The spirit of optimism pervaded all England and, from all reports and dispatches, was also taking possession of the Allied

Nations. Our armies had swept through Normandy; Paris had been occupied, and the German armies were in retreat or in rout. Men and officers were making pools on the date of the German collapse and, everywhere, every one's morale was high. The very next day Anthony Eden gave me the welcome news that, for the first time in five years, the blackout would be lifted and the lights would go on in London. I had called on Mr. Eden in the Foreign Office where Lord Grey, on the eve of the outbreak of World War I, had said: "The lights are going out all over Europe and they will not be rekindled in our time." But on that day with Mr. Eden, it looked as if the lights turned on in London would be the pilot light of proximate Allied victory.

Impetus was given to my own optimism when I visited General Doolittle at his headquarters and was witness to the evidence of the overwhelming power and effectiveness of our Air Forces. It was good to be with General Doolittle again. He seems never to be able to do enough for a person, and though he is a General, one instinctively calls him "Jimmy," and he likes it. A little heavier than when last I saw him in Tunisia, he was still brimful of energy and the source of the spirit that animates the Air Force. He gets full devotion and full service from his staff, and they not only work with him at headquarters—but also live with him.

General Doolittle had just completed a film for President Roosevelt and Mr. Churchill which vividly portrayed the activities and achievements of the Air Forces. The cameras that took the pictures were in the very planes that went out on strategic missions to destroy plants producing war material, lines of communication and supply dumps. There were also pictures taken on tactical missions supporting operations of ground troops, bombing gun positions, and strafing convoys. So realistic were the pictures that I almost felt as if I myself were in the plane and were experiencing the same emotions. But the pictures that we saw told only a portion of the story, for they were taken from the planes that returned!

General Doolittle knows everything about aviation from the ground up to the sky. He is an engineer, a scientist and an administrator, as well as a great aviator, and apparently the master as well as jack of all trades.

I visited many units of the Eighth and Ninth Air Forces and talked with many of the men, and as they showed me scoreboards of their missions and explained their successes, I saw reflected in them the same optimism that all England was feeling.

For some of these airmen I celebrated Mass in the renovated stable of an old manor at Kingscliffe, and one of them brought me a handful of letters, the first mail that had caught up with me. Among the letters was one from a mother whose son had been killed on the Anzio beachhead. Many of the letters I receive and the stories that are told to me are like flames of eternal fire, kindled momentarily, flaring forth in immortal expressions. Quoting from them, I know that I am not breaking confidence with those who bared their hearts to me, for I wish only to bequeath to others the strength of spirit they have given to me.

"Mothers' hearts are laid wide open these days by the fear and anxiety for the safety of their sons," this letter said. "I am not proud of the fact that my son had to give up his very young life for greed and avarice, but I *am* proud that he was a good soldier. If this was his mission in life, I know he did it well. Day by day I grow more grateful, thinking God must have loved Louis very much to have lifted him out of the horror and cruelty of war. It is my greatest consolation.

"Another consoling thought is that he died in Italy. If it was in one of those small old Italian towns with the cobbled streets, where the donkey carts go up and down led by a singing peasant, where the skies are bluer than anywhere else in the world, then he is right back where his roots came from. The sod may be blood-soaked now, but one day God will make it verdant and fruitful again. If he gave up his life to help my father's beloved Italy, perhaps this is as it should be. How strangely He weaves the patterns of our lives!

"Now I know why Louis wrote 'As I get close to things, I don't think I'll make the boat home,' and another time he said, 'Some one has to do this job, and remember, Mom, you taught me many are called but few are chosen, and if we follow that thought we can't go wrong!'

"Knowing that he volunteered to go on patrols, I feel humbly proud of this lad of mine, for I know he must have had a very special sort of courage, realizing full well the uncertainty of his return."

From Kingscliffe, I drove out to the Station Hospital at ———— and spent the afternoon visiting with the patients and doctors. Some of the wounded in the hospitals are eager to talk and thus ease their physical and mental fears and calm their spiritual conflicts. Others live within themselves, unwilling and unable to be freed from the smothering silence of war's memories that imprisons them. With pity I looked into the hungered eyes of those who could not talk, as inwardly they seemed to drink the tears they could not shed. Some of these were men who carried in their hearts the fear, and often the terrible knowledge, of the infidelity of their wives, and a most fantastic and pathetic story was told me by a wounded lieutenant.

During a battle in Italy, one of his men was struck down and plaintively called to him. Though he should not have left the command of his men at the time, something seemed to draw him to the dying man, who exacted from him a promise. With the bleeding stump of his right arm the soldier pointed a few feet away to the hand that had been shot off, and said: "Send my hand home to my wife!" The officer protested, but the soldier said, "You promised," and died. After the battle, another soldier in the outfit told the officer that his buddy was neither crazy nor delirious, and that he doubtless really had wished that his wife might have the hand that he had given her in marriage, for she had been unfaithful to him. That woman will never know the bitter torments she caused this boy who gave his devotion and his life to her and for his country!

I watched the doctors and enlisted personnel of the hospital tend the sick with a gentleness and understanding that could have been born only of faith in God and love of their fellowmen. The medics do not fight with arms, but fight they do, in every theatre of war, to save and soothe their men; and in the field they carry litters of wounded many miles through danger zones of shell-spattered, mine-pitted country, when ambulances and jeeps are unavailable. Their service to the wounded is timeless and tireless.

To the hearts, heads and hands of our doctors is entrusted God's most precious and most wasted gift—human life. Thrust into theatres of war where mass destruction of human bodies, mass snarlings and derangements of human minds are wrought with a magnitude and ruthlessness never known before, the doctor's role and his relation to mankind remain the same: to construct and reconstruct human minds and human bodies. They not only serve their country and their fellowmen, but know the enduring joy of giving back a husband to a wife, a son to his mother. Through them, lives are saved and suffering softened, and because of them sad hearts learn to hope again. Doctors treat the human body for what it is: sanctuary of life and temple of the soul. They know that while there are many physical and mental variations among men, a common humanity binds all together. Men are inclined to think of the differences that separate them rather than of the bonds that unite them. This is one of the causes and, unfortunately, also one of the effects, of this global war. It is the doctor who recognizes that the hopes and fears, the physical and mental sufferings of all people, spring from the same common humanity, and he knows that death brings the same sorrow to the loved ones of rich and poor, of black and white.

Medicine is one of the permanent pillars of peace. The vocation of a doctor prohibits him from erecting racial barriers. The doctor knows only one race—the human race—and his profession meets the challenge of ideal international brotherhood, for the services of a physician, like those of the missionary, are for all men in all places at all times. Doctors make a contract with humanity, exemplifying true democracy in the treatment of human ills, without distinction of color, race or creed.

There may be world-wide confusion about the meaning of democracy, for the word seems to be a deuce-wild in the dictionary and, like penicillin, democracy is considered a specific that can cure all political diseases. But to our men fighting this war there is no better definition of democracy than the Golden Rule whether for nations or for individuals, and while some may call it "trite, wishful thinking" or "utopianism," I know that faith, hope and charity provide the only fertile soil for freedom, the only air in which democracy can breathe, the only axis on which the world can turn in peace.

CHAPTER VI

ADOPTED SOLDIER SONS

WHEN I left England, London was deep in fog, but soon the rain stopped, the fog lifted and the sun came out. We flew over the irregulary plotted, hedge-lined Kentish Weald with its green-and-brown gussets of land in shapes as fantastic as snowflakes. Often, the earth was startlingly scarred with trenches and gun emplacements and pock-marked with fresh and healing war wounds. The Channel was smooth, green and blue; the sky, cloud-spotted, gray and white. This small strip of water, calm as it was that day and flecked with cloud shadows, can be tragically gale-swept and gun-swept. It has borne the argosies of peace, as well as the great armadas of war, and has been, for centuries, England's greatest protection. Fog-covered, it helped England in the days of Dunkirk; sun-drenched, it symbolizes Britain's indomitable spirit. We were only a few minutes flying the Channel and then land, sand, grass, the dark of glen and forest, gray stones, red roofs, and France again!

We circled over the port of Cherbourg massed with boats, over invasion beaches which only a few weeks before had swarmed with boys loving to live, destined to die. But if their destiny was just to die on an invasion beach in life's morning, they died in vain, unless the beachhead of their sacrifice for others was their own bridge to eternal life. The code-name of the shore on which they died was "Omaha," but its real name could be written "Golgotha" for, like the Captain of their souls, these men died that we might live!

79

At the airport I was surprised to meet General John C. H. Lee, whom I had met several times on my previous visit to the war fronts. He has been in charge of our Services of Supply in the European theatre of operations since the beginning of the war. Kindly in manner and thoughtful in act, he took the time and trouble to introduce me to every soldier in the vicinity of the landing place, and accompanied me during the rest of the afternoon on an inspection of Cherbourg, its harbor and its environs. Lest I fear that I was taking him from his duties, he graciously put me at ease, saying that he was on his daily tour of inspection. One quality of greatness attributed to General Lee by those who know and admire him is his desire to have the ablest men in all posts of responsibility, and he himself, with his all-seeing soft blue eyes, makes his own appraisals of results.

While strictly a military man, the General is a soldier of deep religious faith and practice, and he agreed with me that just as patriotism has its full expression in sacrifice and bloodshed, so religion has its real profession in its practice. Something beyond military success is necessary to bridge the chasm between war and peace, and victory through arms alone will not cure the chaos of war. If this were the answer to the war riddle, the puzzle would soon be solved, for our power of construction for destruction is titanic! With the General I visited the elaborate underground tunnels and saw the powerful guns hidden and protected by heavy concrete and rows of camouflaged pillboxes, and the submarine pens that seemed as impregnable to assault from above as would be caverns cut into the Palisades. I watched transports disgorge mountainous masses of weapons for our war machine, and then I saw tangled masses of iron, shattered masonry, the huge ruin of docks and railroads destroyed by war's machinery. This contradiction of construction for destruction struck my heart more sharply because it high-lighted the contrasting elements in the heritage affecting our country's finest and fittest, blighted by the curse of Cain, blessed with the spirit of eternal martyrdom. All our boys who landed, or tried to land, in Normandy on D-Day were victims of this curse, and those who thrust themselves in the line of enemy fire that their buddies on demolition tasks might live for the two minutes necessary to perform their fatal duties were imbued with the spirit of martyrs. And unlesss these scourgings and sufferings awaken us to the realization that God is our Be-all and our End-all, the boys who gave their very young lives on a Normandy beachhead will have died in vain, this war will be won in vain, and the laws of the jungle will continue to prevail!

General Lee, sympathetic and helpful to the chaplains in their work, told me it was a great satisfaction to him to find chaplains of all faiths considerate of one another. I, too, in my journeyings among our soldiers, in camps, in hospitals, on air fields and on the fighting fronts, have been impressed by the spirit of mutal aid and esteem among chaplains of all denominations, and I told the General about Chaplain M——'s experience during the fighting in Italy. The Captain of their regiment was a Catholic, but the Protestant Chaplain did not think him a very good Catholic—and told him so. He talked to him like a Dutch uncle, saying: "You're not only a poor Christian, but a worse Catholic. We have faced the same dangers and shared the same foxhole, and we know that only God in His goodness has kept us unharmed. Now get busy; I'm bringing Father M—— to you!" Good as his word, this Protestant Chaplain brought the Priest to the Captain. When the Captain came through one hundred percent, the Protestant Chaplain murmured, "Thank God!"

It should occasion no surprise to discover evidences of Christian charity motivating the lives and actions of all chaplains; and unless Catholic chaplains were comprehensive in their sympathies, they would not be true to their vocation, whose fundamental tenet is love of God and love of neighbor; and their actions would be in complete variance with the very meaning of "Catholic," which is "broad, universal, impartial, unbigoted."

At the headquarters of General Lee, I again met General John L. DeWitt, still in the service though past the age of retirement. At the beginning of the war he was Commander of our Western Frontier Defense, responsible for all military organizations from the Aleutians to the Panama Canal. Later, he went to Washington as head of the War College, and when General McNair was killed last July in France he took over his assignment.

General DeWitt, a soldier all his life, comes from a family of soldiers. Memories of the last war's recoil, the futility of its peace, his emotion at fighting again on soil irrigated with the blood of America's sons have made him warlike for the sake of peace. Recognizing that our problems in this war are far greater than they were in the first world war, as well as vastly more complicated and world-wide in scope, he spoke with the greatest admiration of the strength, courage, skill and equipment of the American Armies. This praise and appraisal by General DeWitt were confirmed by my own stirring experience the following day, when an American officer who had had an important role in planning and executing the operation that established the "Omaha" beachhead described in detail the events of D-Day. On the shore of the beach he spread out a large map of the entire area and explained the intricate and conflicting problems involved in the co-ordination of land, sea and air forces. To be successful, everything connected with the preliminary action had to take place within one half hour. The tide had to be high enough for the landing craft to clear the rocks, and not too high to prevent demolition detachments from destroying the shore defenses of steel and rock. Some yards back of the high-water line, cliffs rose precipitously and the whole area was strongly defended by tank traps, trenches and guns of various types. While this beach was not the most favorable one for a landing, it was chosen because it provided an element of surprise to the enemy.

The Colonel wished me to understand not only what was planned but also what actually happened, so he took me out into the harbor in a "Duck," and I saw the shoreline as our American soldiers and sailors saw it on that morning of D-Day. The Germans had been alerted some five hours before the landing. Stormy, cloudy weather prevented air support and there was a choppy, churning sea; but despite every obstacle, our objectives were reached, due, the Colonel said with quiet pride in his voice, to the bravery and moral force of the American soldier, his leadership, training and equipment. Each soldier knew what he was to do, and nearly all of those among the first waves died in the doing. Row on row they fell, struck with the thud of death, making "the first successful landing in history on a heavily defended beach." Describing the operation in his soft, steeled voice, the Colonel, who had been in one of the foremost boats and was its lone survivor, relived, as his words pictured it for me, that victorious, costly day. Many of the men had lived twenty, twenty-five and thirty years for this D-Day, and it became for them their birthday in Eternity. Now their bodies rest on the plateau above the beach, immortalized in history and immortal in eternal glory. Over this beachhead have now passed more than a million American soldiers, and each one of them has seen an arch which bears the inscription, "Along this trail has passed the pride of the American Armed Forces."

Leaving the Cherbourg area on my way to visit General Eisenhower I passed through Coutances, or at least what had once been Coutances, for this city, like so many others in Normandy, lies in complete ruin. The cathedral alone remains, and it, only because of the courage and initiative of one old priest. When the Americans reached Coutances, they believed Germans were still in the town and continued their shelling. Waving a white handkerchief, this priest ran out toward the soldiers, told them the Germans had left the city, and offered himself as a hostage to be shot if his words were not true. The soldiers followed him into the town, found the Germans had fled, and today the cathedral stands unharmed in the midst of destruction—a symbol of resurrection to enkindle the fire of faith and of regeneration among the people of France.

At Headquarters, General Eisenhower greeted me in his office caravan. It was seventeen months since last I had seen him, and during that period the war had made great progress in its stride towards victory. General Eisenhower's face is still youthful; his skin, sunburned rather than tanned; and though the wrinkles in his forehead have deepened, his entire physical and mental bearing gives the impression of a man hardened and, at the same time, resilient as a rapier. Gravely aware of his tremendous personal responsibility in spending human lives to gain military objectives, the General was concerned not with the victories that had been won, but with the gigantic tasks that were ahead; and even our brilliant military successes had not created in him unwarranted feelings of optimism, though he was supremely confident of the ultimate complete success of his plans and operations. He did not think that Germany's collapse was imminent and it was from the General that I first heard the word "winter"! After that, it hurt my heart when boys asked me if I thought the war would be over by Christmas.

In General Eisenhower's trailer, nestled in an apple orchard sloping down to the Bay of St. Malo, I met Air Marshal Tedder, Deputy Chief of Staff, and General Walter Beadle Smith, the General's Chief of Staff. Air Marshal Tedder is a man of medium stature, his face rather thin and pale, his eyes very dark brown. To me, the most surprising thing about him was his mild, almost meek, manner; but there is nothing small, mild or meek about his accomplishments, for his reputation as a master of strategy and tactics in air warfare is of the highest. General Smith did not appear to have aged at all. During my two days at Headquarters I had several visits with him and even in the midst of exacting and responsible duties, and at the end of a hard and tiring day, he still seemed fresh and full of energy. He is incisive in speech and act; to him, directing and commanding are second nature. Of average height and physique, he was evidently in top physical condition, and strength and power showed in his every action. His brown eyes too, are brilliant and full of vitality.

One mid-afternoon, I walked alone through this apple orchard with its trees heavily freighted with fruit, through pine groves and fields, to visit a little chapel in a town overlooking the Bay of St. Malo where the Blessed Virgin is venerated under the title of "Our Lady of the Sand Dunes." There with some fisherfolk I knelt, and with them prayed to Mary, deeply and devoutly loved in Normandy, that once more she bless this peaceful land with peace, that she give courage to its people and, above all, that she restore understanding and compassion to the hearts of men.

The following morning on my way to the cemetery at

Ste. Mère l'Eglise, with its acres of graves of Americans who gave their lives in the battles of Normandy, we were stopped by a gathering of French people before the parish church in the square of the little town. The night had been stormy, the morning was shrouded in mist, and the ground wet and muddy. Nevertheless, men, women and children had made a special effort to dress their best, and the little children carried bouquets of flowers. They gathered round me, and the mayor read an address in English. The style was quaint, but its message sincere and, while the people did not understand the words, I think they took some pride in the fact that their mayor spoke my language.

"As Mayor of Ste. Mère l'Eglise," he said, "I have the great honor to welcome you to our city in the name of all the population. You have come from one of the largest towns in the world, several thousand miles from France, because your sons are dead on our ground. They are dead because they would prevent the erasure of the word 'freedom' from all human languages. When you return to America, may it please you to tell the mothers and widows who weep for your dead that they have not fallen in vain. Do tell them, also, that they have not fallen on foreign land but on friendly soil, and that French mothers and wives will tend their graves, and on Sundays they will go to the cemetery and honor them with prayers and flowers. Soon, each French family of the town is going to adopt the heroes who lie buried here, exactly as if they were their own sons, and as a sacred duty they will pray at their graves for their souls.

"My country has been plundered by two horrible wars in one generation. She has had her homes devastated, and we have seen growing from our ground whole fields of wooden crosses. Almighty God has chosen France to show the evils that man's pride and ambition have caused the whole world, for men from all parts of the world now sleep in the earth of France. They have given their youth, their future, their hopes and their love, so that instead of 'Heil Hitler,' people might say without fear, 'Our Father Who art in Heaven, deliver us from evil.'"

Shortly after Mass in the cemetery, I continued on my way. We circled Mont-St.-Michel, fantastic rocky isle of Gothic beauty in the Bay of St. Malo, and flew above Avranches and St. Lô, so flattened that I could see from one end of the town to the other. We flew also over Falaise towards Lisieux with its Carmelite convent and the basilica enshrining the body of St. Theresa—the humble nun known throughout the world as "The Little Flower." "Lisieux must not be another Cassino," was the fevered, fervent cry of all who lived in Lisieux, of all who loved its saint. This town had been liberated by the British Army and, in its more than a dozen bombings, over a thousand townspeople were killed and there were bodies still lying under the ruins. Today in Lisieux little remains standing except the basilica erected to the memory of the Little Flower, the cathedral which in its twelfth century grace rises out of the surrounding shambles, and the convent where St. Theresa took her vows fifty-five years ago.

Many Carmelite nuns were outside their convent for the first time since taking their vows of silence and invisibility, among them two sisters of the Little Flower. One of them, Mother Agnes, left the cloister for the first time in sixty years to help care for the homeless and helpless who were sheltered in the convent grounds. While all the Carmelite nuns miraculously escaped unharmed, twenty nuns of another community were found dead beneath the rubble of the Benedictine Abbey of Notre Dame after a bomb had made a direct hit and set it aflame.

The cathedral bells of Lisieux tolled the deaths of thirteen Little Sisters of the Poor and of the sixty old men in their care, killed when their home for the aged was bombed and burned. The ways of war are merciless!

The Normans are a frugal, courageous people and are doing their best to help themselves, but their poverty and immense sufferings have driven them to beg from others the commonest necessities of life: a bit of food, a little wood or coal, a piece of soap, or even rags to serve as towels and handkerchiefs. "Don't cry," one little girl of Lisieux said to her companion; "you can't get another handkerchief."

On our way to Paris we flew over the villages and towns of Normandy with the dark green of their trees and hedges framing the lighter green of grass and gardens. The dome of the Church of the Sacré Coeur of Montmartre, haloed in cloud, was the first building of Paris that we recognized. Soon we landed at Le Bourget Airport and observed the effects of the fury of American bombings. Hangars were masses of tangled steel and blasted concrete, and great, deep holes cratered the field.

The last time I had been in Paris was in 1932. It was just before my consecration as bishop, when I was secretary to Cardinal Lauri returning from the Eucharistic Congress in Dublin, and the home of the Cardinal Archbishop, the last place I had visited in Paris on that occasion, was the first place to which I now returned. Cardinal Suhard and others had expected me to arrive in Paris in time for ten o'clock Mass on Sunday morning in the Cathedral of Notre Dame. Utterly ignorant of these plans, I had said Mass for American soldiers on Sunday morning in the middle of a cornfield, and it had seemed like the middle of the night, for it was cold, dark and dreary. When I reached the Cardinal's residence, he had just returned from the cathedral,

where he had celebrated Mass in my stead. Cardinal Suhard
said that no one had announced the substitution, and that one
American soldier leaving Notre Dame after the services had re-
marked, "I wonder why the Archbishop didn't say something to
us; he seemed to have a lot to say every other place he visited!"

Cardinal Suhard is a gentle, venerable priest but his smile
does not completely hide the sadness in his dark eyes. Because
of his strong representations to, and protests against, the Nazis,
he was their victim. Returning from the Basilica of the Sacred
Heart of Montmartre one morning about a week after the German occupation of Paris, he found two Nazi officers awaiting
him. He received them in the large parlor of his home, and he
received them standing! The Germans ordered the Cardinal into
the dining room, closeted ten other priests in an adjoining room,
forbade them to talk to one another, placed guards at every door
and disconnected the telephones. They offered luncheon to the
Cardinal but he refused it because it had been denied to his
priests. The Cardinal's home and the chancery next door were
ransacked from garret to cellar. The sacristy was sealed, and no
one was to touch the seals "under pain of death." The Cardinal
was deprived of the privilege of saying daily Mass but, insisting,
he was finally told that he could do so on Sunday morning at
eight-thirty. Sunday came but when he was ready for service
the guard told him he could not leave his room until the Captain
had arrived. That night at six-thirty the Cardinal was still fast-
ing, but the Captain had not come.

What was gained? Nothing. The mounds of documents
carted away by the Nazis were of no importance to them. And
from Cardinal Suhard they gained only his continued refusal
to receive the leader of French Naziism; his repeated protests

against the persecution, massacre and deportation of the Jews; his constant demands for humane treatment for hostages. When questioned regarding his allegiances, he replied: "As a bishop I have defended inalienable rights. As a French bishop I have done my duty towards my country. No one can make me express regret for having defended these rights or fulfilled these duties. If I made any other declaration I would not expect you to believe that it was sincere. Therefore you can demand of me respect for the armistice, but you need demand nothing contrary to my faith as an Archbishop or to my status as a Frenchman. You will obtain nothing."

These words brought to my memory Cardinal Mercier when he visited America after his country's and his own liberation from the Germans. Over the span of years the memorable occasion was clearly pictured in my mind, for I was a newly ordained priest on the cathedral staff when, for the first time on American soil, Cardinal Mercier met King Albert of Belgium, in the Cathedral of the Holy Cross in Boston. Cardinal Mercier said that he never stopped to consider whether the consequences of any action of his would be good or harmful to himself, but to friends and enemies he spoke the truth as he saw it, cared for his people as best he could, and left himself to the care of God. And the Cardinal's reference to patriotism has ever stayed with me. "Patriotism," he said, "is not a mere word. It is a deep reality, a principle of life."

I left Cardinal Suhard's house with Chaplain Grady who, after serving many months with our troops in Normandy where his only church was a "cathedral in the mud," suddenly, surprisingly found himself in charge of American services in the famous Church of the Madeleine in Paris. We went there together to meet some of our soldiers, and afterwards I drove out of Paris along the main highway towards Le Mans, where I heard an amusing story that might have been a tragic one, were it not for the presence of mind of a French farmer. To escape from the Gestapo, a priest disguised himself as a servant, and took refuge in a farmhouse. One evening, just at supper time, two Nazi soldiers arrived seeking the priest. The farmer admitted that there might be a priest hidden there that he knew nothing about. "You must do your duty," he said. "Search the place." Then, turning to the priest, he ordered, "Take the lantern and go with these gentlemen through the house and barn and let them look into every corner." The Germans found no priest. Just as they were leaving, the "servant" said, "Please don't forget the poor domestic," and one of the soldiers, giving him a five-franc note, said, "Thanks for carrying the lantern." And the disguised priest answered, "My pleasure, Sir!"

The roadway to Le Mans had felt the tread of millions fleeing from the terrors of the Nazi torture-machine. In wretched wagons drawn by panting horses, on bicycles and in ox-drawn carts they fled, while streams of civilians pulled their own carts and in their arms carried children pathetically hugging broken toys and tattered dolls, children whose hearts, almost like the Christ Child's, began to break as soon as they began to beat. One hunted, haunted mother pushed a carriage along the roadway with two little girls in it—and both of them were dead!

There are countless stories of the systematic starvation, of the brutalities and barbaric tortures endured in concentration camps, and in all these devastated countries there are few homes into which the blood-dripping hands of fiendish Nazi invaders have not reached. The heart-crushing statistics of these plundered lands reveal war's cardinal crime, the crime against war's children:

We do not sense the toll of war, the price
Man pays for putting faith in force of arms,
Till we have seen war's children and their woe.
They are our generation's sacrifice
For immolation on the altars raised,
Not to the loving fatherhood of God,
But to the cold and cruel cult of Mars.
Dragons' teeth are seed for children, sired
For War's brute reaping. Cycle without end!
Once more, it is the innocent who die.

The casualties among children from forced malnutrition and enforced slavery have been greater than those on the fields of battle. It is one of war's most terrifying thoughts that countless thousands of these children, who will become the guardians of the peace, have lost more than health and energy—they have lost the very will to honesty and decency. They have become wolf-children, predatory and skilled in deceit in foraging for the necessities of life. Since the occupation, over a million children subsisting at famine level have died in France, and three-quarters of Belgium's children are pre-tubercular from lack of food. Poland's tragedy has been the greatest, for more than half of her eleven million children under fifteen years of age have been liquidated by starvation or enslavement, and many are tooth-less because of the calcium-deficiency of the mothers who bore them. Many of those who survived were used to supply blood for the enemy wounded, and when drained of life were buried in nameless pits.

Leaders of nations large and small proclaim their passionate desire for an abiding peace. They list the vast and varied labors that will be required to restore economic balance to their countries. Topping the list should be the flesh-and-blood welfare of the children of these nations. Without health assurance for them, as the primary requirement, all other safeguards of the peace will be short-lived. Until I had witnessed creeping death spreading over the occupied countries after the invasion of hunger, I never realized the full meaning of the slogan, "Food will win the war and write the peace." The long denial of adequate food has so arrested brain-tissue development in children that mental growth has been stunted. This means that the surviving children will have the bodies of adults but the minds of children, and will be fitted only for unskilled pursuits, destined for lives of limited horizons. Lands may be reclaimed, cities may be rebuilt, but the starved bodies of children cannot be restored.

They are no wild dreamers, who say that a bottle of milk will do more good than a book of speeches. They are not under-selling America who say that we must share in providing these desolate peoples with the munitions of peace—food, clothing and medical supplies—for peace will not thrive among nations in a world where half are well-fed and the rest are half-starved. To millions of children democracy is still only a word and a promise. They have been exposed to hatred, hunger and a hopeless future, and if they are denied the right to take their places in a world of personal security, they will form the underground army for the next war, and take by stealth and force what they cannot enjoy by right.

Conferences on monetary stabilization, the control of cartels and the levelling of trade barriers are important, but the essential conferences are those that will write a real Declaration of Opportunity, insuring strong minds and strong bodies for the children who will be the trustees of the peace. Children are the cheapest commodity of war, but the most precious element of an enduring peace. They are the seed of tomorrow. We must provide them with life-giving soil!

> Somewhere—the place it matters not—somewhere
> I saw a child, hungry and thin of face—
> Eyes in whose pools life's joy no longer stirred,
> Lips that were dead to laughter's eager kiss,
> Yet parted fiercely to a crust of bread.
> And since that time I walk in ceaseless fear,
> Fear that the child I saw, and all the hosts
> Of children in a world at play with death,
> May die; or living, live in bitterness.
> O God, today, above the cries of war,
> Hear Thou Thy children's prayer, and grant to us
> Thy peace, God's peace—
>   and bread for starving children!

The Mass I offered for American troops in the Palace of Versailles was an historic occasion because it was the first time in nearly a century that Mass had been celebrated in the chapel. And another historic occasion—at least for me—was when I had the temerity to speak French in the Cathedral of Notre Dame! Twice was I privileged to celebrate Mass in this cathedral, once privately and once on a solemn occasion in thanksgiving for the liberation of Paris. Cardinal Suhard presided at this ceremony, and the vast historic fane, the center, the heart and the hope of France, was thronged with American soldiers. The full choir sang extraordinarily beautiful music, and when the organ played the "Star-Spangled Banner," I realized that, though I had been with Americans every day, this was the first occasion on which I had heard my national anthem since leaving home.

In thanking Cardinal Suhard and the French people I spoke

French, but I had made up my mind that even if I were at a loss for something to say I would not mention Lafayette and Rochambeau, for Bob Murphy had told me that no American ever put three sentences together in public in France without referring to these men. But the Cardinal must have thought I had forgotten them, for after I had finished my talk he spoke of both of them in his. I am sure that none of the teachers who tried to teach me French grammar, including the use of the subjunctive, which I studiously learned to avoid, could ever have imagined that I would some day speak French in the great Cathedral of Notre Dame!

In one of the many churchyard cemeteries that I visited I saw evidences of the thoughtful gratitude of the French Underground to our American soldiers, graves decorated with plain wooden crosses, inscribed: "Here lies the body of an unknown American airman shot down over this village. He died for France. May he rest in peace!" These graves were well-kept and covered with a few fresh field flowers, and the feeling of the French mothers is tenderly expressed in a prayer for our soldiers that Father Keenan gave me when he told me about the celebration of Mother's Day here in Normandy. When he arrived to celebrate Mass in the first American cemetery of the American First Army, over a thousand men, women and children were already there, the men standing on the right and the women on the left fringe of the graves. Boys and girls, all carrying in their arms bouquets of red roses, stood in front and in back of the mounds headed with their white wooden Crosses and Stars of David. Our American soldiers knelt directly in front of the altar decorated with candles and vases of red roses, in the center of the cemetery. At either side were two immense floral wreaths, one: "To Our Liberators," and the other: "To the Mothers of Our Liberators." The Stars and Stripes, the Tricolor and the Union Jack, all homemade by the French, blended to form the back-drop of the altar.

The French men and women sang the entire Mass as they had been taught to do from childhood. It was an ideal summer day, the sun momentarily touching everything and every one with its light and peace. The messages of the Mayor and of the French priest, a chaplain in the last World War, were of love and gratitude and prayer for our soldier-dead, and for their soldier-mothers who gave their sons that France and the world might be free. France would never forget. Her debt would be paid in priceless prayer for the heroic American mothers and for their martyred sons in France. While the last verses of the "Magnificat" were being sung, French mothers placed full-blown red roses upon the graves while fervently they recited a prayer:

"Dear American Soldier, buried far away from home in our French earth, rest in peace. We will care for you. We love and thank you. We love your mother and we thank her, too. I, also, am a mother. I know what it means to suffer the pangs of giving birth, of loving my son and then losing him in total war. Permit me to do for you what your own dear mother would do if she were here. My rose upon your grave is her rose also. It tells in words of mother-love how proud we are, how grateful, yes, how glad we are, even in our tears, for the life given you, that you might give that life to Freedom and to God. My rose also means rosary, and one rosary after another I shall offer to the Mother of the mothers of soldiers that they may find solace and strength in the Heart of Mary, the Comfortress of the Afflicted."

Returning to Paris through the picturesque countryside I was thinking of the cheapness of human life and the continued decimation of men. Contrary to the rule that scarceness increases value, human life daily grows cheaper. In the very center of

Paris I saw a half-dozen boys in their middle teens with rifles across their knees seated beneath a great sign which read: "Young French Communist Organization," and autos of the French Forces of the Interior, daubed "F.F.I.," driven madly through the streets by armed youngsters. The wildest wild west tales are child's-play compared with today's realities. A blight has come over mankind, stunning human reason, callousing human feel-ings, deadening human hearts.

War is a toughening, hardening, brutalizing process, not alone to the human body, but to human sensibilities and the human spirit as well. It may so harden a man that he can, with-out flinching, shoot others, or so soften him that he will shoot himself. When men see bestial atrocities committed before their very eyes; when they hold their buddies in their arms and feel their life's blood ebb away; when they watch planes disintegrate in the air, and see the twisted, tortured frames of boys they respect and admire, there comes instinctively the passion for revenge. Our boys fighting this war were born rational, normal human beings; thousands of them have said they are "fighting to get home," and I pray they will be able to get home before the process of war brutalizes the human and rational in them, before they learn to love fighting for its own sake.

One youngster pilot said to me: "When you come through a stream of searing shell-fire alive and you hope and pray your buddy is safe too; and then you find him with a hole where his heart should be; when you help dig his grave with the shovel you always carry with you, and bury him in the mattress-cover-shroud he always carried with him—it doesn't make for tranquil-lity or love; it makes you want to 'get' the guy who 'got' your buddy." It is heartrending that, in war, hate begets hate, and smothers right and reason.

When I reached my quarters in Paris a French official was waiting for me to ask my help in obtaining information about two thousand French civilian prisoners who had been deported. They had all been herded into a train, as many as sixty to a freight car without even a wisp of straw to lie on, and during a night in mid-August had been taken away. He knew that the men had been interned in a concentration camp near Weimar, but it had been impossible to get any information whatever concerning the four hundred women deported at the same time. The officer wished to locate the place to which these unfortunate women had been sent so that at least an attempt could be made to get some food and clothing through to them. This was only one of the stories that I heard day after day, almost hour after hour, deepening in me the realization that the dikes of hate and lust have been breached, deluging mankind with human woe.

Man has become contemptuous not alone of the lives of others, but often of his own. Two youths in their early twenties proved this contempt of human life when they priced their own lives at two dollars each and acted as German spies within the American lines. The information which they gave to the enemy was responsible for American deaths and, justly, they were condemned to die. To die for two dollars each! I remember the incident in detail because of other circumstances connected with these boys. They were born on the same day, in the same town, on the same street. They had always been pals. On the same day, in the same place, in the same way, they died—but not at the same moment. For, although they were standing together unblindfolded, the guns of one firing squad had not been loaded and, after the first volley, one boy, still smoking a cigarette, remained standing—until the next volley!

My visit with General de Gaulle was the first one of the day. I arrived early at his office in the Ministry of War and was talking with his secretary when the General came in, greeted me and brought me into his office with the informality and cordiality of an American businessman. Strong men make strong enemies as well as strong friendships. General de Gaulle has many ardent champions and many, even among his own countrymen, who are opposed to him. He has consistently and steadily grown in stature, and at the present time the fearless, determined General has the support of the great majority of his own people in France, as well as of Frenchmen throughout the world, for they realize that he symbolizes their hopes for the unity and resurrection of France.

General de Gaulle is a stalwart, stable, soldiery character; he knows what he wants; and he thinks that what he wants is best for his country. He also says what he wants and thinks, and his faculty for expressing his ideas directly and decisively with a minimum of words makes him sound at times almost curt. He does not accept the opinions of others if these opinions are at variance with his own convictions. An American General who knows General de Gaulle well said to me: "I like the General. I do not believe he is always right, but I believe he thinks he is. He always has his feet on the ground, he knows what the score is, and he is as sincere as the morning sun." I have seen General de Gaulle now many times during the past three years, in London, Africa, America, and finally in his own France, and each time I have found him stronger and more positive in his leadership and power.

France is paying reverence to her Allies who fought and died upon her soil; the French people are making every effort humanly possible to help themselves, and General de Gaulle is making

every effort to guide them and get aid for them. But France is
tired, with millions of her men killed, maimed, enslaved in vile
concentration camps or forced to labor in Hitler's frantic factories
—and we must help France to help herself if the world is to have
the grace of a durable peace.

Shortly after my visit to General de Gaulle I met a Frenchman from Limoges who told me about Oradour, "place of prayer"
—the Lidice of France—ghost-town of horror, pillage and massacre, with every one of its fifteen hundred villagers dead! It was
one more pathetic proof of the pitiful plight and dire need of
the people of France. When the Nazi troops arrived in Oradour,
they said they had information that arms were hidden in the
vicinity, and ordered the men, women and children into the
church and neighboring barns for verification of their papers.
Unafraid because they were not guilty, the villagers soberly and
quietly did as they were told. Over five hundred women and
children, some of them from the neighboring towns of Limoges
and Lorraine, were there—and all marched into the church and
the barns which became their funeral pyres, for the Nazis had
stored explosives in the church! The barns and the church were
set afire. Terrified, the children called frantically to their dying,
suffocating mothers, helpless in their torture. And any one who
tried to escape was machine-gunned.

Every house in the village was put to flame. The church was
a scene of ghastly horror, and in the rectory garden were empty
baby-carriages in which mothers had unsuspectingly brought
their babies to the slaughter. One survivor whose entire family
was murdered could only murmur in his heart-shattering sorrow:
"I offer my prayers and this sacrifice for the redemption of souls
throughout the world and for the salvation of France."

Nor is it unusual throughout France to hear of people who

are suffering the extremes of misery offering prayers and sacrifice for her salvation. In the small town of Cornimont in the Vosges Mountains where for four years the people lived within range of the German guns, some five hundred villagers prayed daily in a dark, damp cellar where the pastor, whose church had been shelled into ruins, made this announcement: "We are experiencing all kinds of hardships—hunger, cold and fear, and it could hardly be called weakness to ask Gor for release from these evils. But if the hour has not yet come for us to be heard, let us offer this hunger, this cold and this fear, for the salvation of France."

Such is the spirit of these French people, drawn so closely together by common sufferings that even the outrageous indignities heaped upon them by the Nazis cannot shatter their faith. One little room in which I slept had a Crucifix over the door and a framed inscription: "Bear each other's heartaches, for the time is short that you will be together."

Oftentimes cynically, unbelievers, half-believers and believers have asked me: "Is there anything for us to be thankful for? Should we be thankful for years of relentless carnage, for the ruin of our country, the slaughter of our children, the persecution and deaths of our dear ones?" No! But we must be thankful for the courage that keeps alive within us the flame of faith in one another and in God. We must be thankful for the courage and faith of boys like Sergeant De Franzo, the first boy from Saugus, Massachusetts, to die in action, killed in the deadly hedgerows of France while clearing a blazing path through concentrated enemy fire. For this action of "selfless heroism and calculated sacrifice," he was posthumously awarded our nation's highest award for valor, the Congressional Medal of Honor. One of his officers said: "Arthur knew he would draw enough fire to kill off a whole battalion, but he knew too that he could save the lives of most of his company."

And because of the courage and faith of all our boys and because of their faith in us, I ask in their name for a just and sane peace which is the only kind that will safeguard America from the future sacrifice of hundreds of thousands of other Arthur de Franzos.

CHAPTER VII

WITH THREE OF OUR FOUR STARS

O N my way to General Bradley's headquarters I stopped at the Cathedral of Notre Dame, and even in the dimness of dawn I could see where its doors had been bullet-spattered by machine guns, only a few days before, when General de Gaulle had gone there to offer prayers of thanksgiving for the liberation of France. Leaving Paris, I drove along the banks of the Seine and then, instead of keeping to the direct route, I followed the Marne, for I wished to stop in prayer for our boys at Château-Thierry, Soissons and Rheims, towns reminiscent of 1914. Throughout France, you could almost guess the time of liberation of the towns from the kind of greeting you received. If the Americans had just reached a place, the people would be grouped in doorways or on sidewalks, clapping, laughing, waving, throwing flowers and even crying for joy; but if some days had elapsed, the people walking along the streets simply made the victory sign. They quickly became accustomed to us, and ignorance of each other's language was no barrier to friendliness. Over and over again the same villages, towns and cities have suffered from periodic eruptions of war, and when a Red Cross worker said to me at Château-Thierry, "My father died here," I realized that these eruptions have now overflowed into America. On bodies, in hearts, and even upon the earth's face, scars from the last war have not yet healed, and again mankind hangs crucified by human hates.

In the half-light of the morning we passed convoys with

their precious supplies, troops in trucks, tanks and tank-destroyers, all streaming forward. The young drivers—their faces haggard and bearded, their eyes red-rimmed and tired, their arms and hands numbed—were grimly keeping pace with the moving front. Crippled German tanks and trucks were scattered all along the roadside, and in the fields crashed planes lay lifeless after their death-dealing missions.

In the Cathedral City of Rheims, I stopped to call on the Archbishop and to see the Cathedral which still bears the name "Tears of Rheims" from its festoons of melted lead, war wounds of 1914. As I walked about the city and saw new scars, I could not know that before the end of another war-year, this historic City of Rheims would be the scene of the "unconditional surrender" of the enemy who caused the ruins of two terrible World Wars.

I arrived at General Bradley's headquarters on the day that he was conferring with the Commanding Generals of the Twelfth Army Group, and with him I met General Courtney H. Hodges of the First Army and General George S. Patton, Jr., of the Third Army. Before the conference began, however, I had the opportunity of being alone with General Bradley for more than an hour. One entire side of his van was covered with a very large, brightly lighted map of the war zone, indicating the dispositions of all the Allied and enemy forces. Patiently he explained to me the progress of the campaign, from the landings in Normandy to the position of the armies on that day, detailing possible future moves and their advantages, difficulties and dangers. We sat on chairs before the map and as the places discussed were high or low on it, we stood up or sat down, and moved our chairs along as the story developed. As the General described movements of troops he would place his open hand on the map in a gesture as if actually to transport a unit from one place to another.

General Bradley, the first member of his class to become a General, was graduated with General Eisenhower from West Point Military Academy in the Class of 1915, and General Eisenhower says that he still thinks General Bradley the best General of the class. Though he had never been in France before, so wide and accurate is General Bradley's knowledge of geography, history, terrain and everything pertaining to war, that to me it seemed as if he had lived there all his life— preparing for it. Competent military men say that his ability as a military tactician in modern warfare is unsurpassed and have called him the outstanding figure on the western battle front. One General said to me: "General Bradley has proved himself to be great by every military standard; he is also a great human being, and if the great Generals of this war must be numbered on the fingers of one hand, General Bradley must be one of them."

With the ports of Brittany still occupied by the enemy, General Bradley had his army turn its back on its supply line and strike towards the east and Paris. For, although Cherbourg was in Allied hands, it could not then be effectively used as a port and General Bradley had to depend on supplies brought over the beaches. General Grant had done something equally bold when he abandoned his supply line and had his army live on whatever it could forage from the country, but this was the first time since Vicksburg that a General had dared this maneuver. After the break-through our armies moved with such incredible speed that General Bradley, suspecting that the Germans did not have sufficient reserves for the counterattack they were making, waited twenty-four hours to be convinced of that fact, and then sent his troops around the right flank to the rear of the Germans, and the Americans continued to plunge ahead.

Quiet, aggressive, determined, General Bradley never raises his voice above a conversational tone. His attitude and actions reminded me of a college professor, and certainly the van, with its chairs, pads of paper, pencils, map, blackboard and pointer, looked like a schoolroom. While the General and I were in the van I heard the strangest noises on the roof. It sounded as if some little boys were playing leap-frog there and as if others were bouncing balls. I could not imagine what the racket was all about and finally I asked the General. "Oh," he said, "those are my two dogs playing. They climb up the camouflage net like monkeys and have a great time together!"

I was standing with General Bradley and General Hodges when General Patton arrived. I heard General Patton warmly congratulate General Hodges on his achievement of being the first General to invade Germany since Napoleon. Both Generals cordially invited me to visit their troops and it was arranged that I should go first to the Third Army. I flew up to General Patton's headquarters in a small plane which took off from a very rough field—so rough that one of the tires burst on the take-off. The air surveillance was naturally very rigid, and since it was a bit foggy, the pilot was continually sweeping the sky with his eyes. While no hostile planes appeared, it was disconcerting even when friendly planes zoomed towards us for investigation. We ran into bad weather and the rain never beat any harder against the old barn roof than it beat against the glass front of that plane; and rain beating on the windshield of a plane runs up and over, instead of down and out! But we got where we were going.

General Patton, an unusually tall man, makes a striking

figure as he strides along, straight and as supple as a sapling. He is many-sided and vari-gifted, and although he claims to be nothing but a soldier, any prolonged conversation with him reveals that he is extremely well informed in many fields other than the military. He is frank and outspoken even on first acquaintance, and frankness is a most engaging quality.

During the days I was with the Third Army I spent much time with General Patton in many places and under many circumstances. I even stayed up late at night with him, which was the one thing I did as well as he. General Patton is a driver, but he drives himself first and hardest. He said that his soldiers travelled so fast that the Chaplains with his army couldn't even see the Cathedral of Chartres as they passed—and added that General Bradley himself was so hard pressed that he could not take time out to visit Château-Thierry when he was only a few miles away.

The General told me a story about a soldier who, having decided that he had had enough fighting, was working his way towards the rear, and who, when in the dark he was challenged, answered: "Yes, Lieutenant!" only to hear the voice angrily growl: "Lieutenant!" The soldier tried again: "Excuse me, Captain," and again the voice impatiently barked: "Captain!" The same procedure rapidly followed, through "Major" and "Colonel," until finally the disgusted voice from the darkness said: "Don't you recognize a General when you meet one?" Appalled, the soldier exclaimed, "Am I that far back!" That story has no application to General Patton, who "is always in some Purple Heart alley, where he and the enemy are looking down each other's throats." The General spends much time up front among his troops because he believes a commander should lead and inspire his men, and the frequent bombings of his own headquarters contradict the jocose statement that there must be a gentleman's agreement among enemy commanders not to bomb one another. General Patton himself thinks that the brave man is he who voluntarily faces danger when justifiably he could be safe, for, he said, man not only fears death, but fears even to be hurt.

Another side of the General was revealed to me when he spoke affectionately of a ninety-six-year-old lady, Miss Mary Scally, who had cared for him in his infancy and childhood. For more than ten years she has been bedridden in a hospital in Los Angeles, and now it is he who cares for her.

General Patton and General Hugh Gaffey, his able, silver-haired, serious-faced Texan Chief of Staff, arranged my visits to various units, including one that, only the day before, had pushed across the Moselle River. Any consolation that one can bring to our boys pays infinite dividends in self-satisfaction, and I wanted to go any place where the Generals or Chaplains felt I might bring the slightest comfort to the men. Whatever other weapons, known or secret, America may have, the greatest one will always be the American Boy. It is a revelation to see the way he adapts himself to the hardships of war. I saw and talked with boys just arrived, boys who were for the first time outside the United States, who had forded their first river, seen the first of their own buddies killed and wounded, and were already veterans. They looked like high-school youngsters, and some had scarcely begun to shave. In these formative years when they would normally be enriching their minds through schooling, strengthening their bodies through sports and recreation, developing their characters through home influences, these boys are being disciplined only by the hardships, heartaches and hurts of war.

In an old battered barn I found several of these lads huddled together writing letters home by the light of a single candle. One youngster said to me half seriously, half facetiously, but nevertheless earnestly: "I hope that Jerry right over there on the hill won't make a direct hit tonight. They've been at it ever since I landed here. But right behind us are our mortars and artillery, and they'll answer them! So I figure I'm pretty safe for a while, at least until I finish this letter to Dad—I hope!" So young, so far away from home, under constant fire, and so typically American!

One of the other lads had just finished a letter. It was not to *his* mother and dad, but to the mother and father of his pal, who had been shot down only one week after landing. "I know this letter won't cushion the blow or soften the pain in your heart," he wrote, "because I know how my mother felt when she lost her youngest son only seven months ago. Yet I want you to know how we all felt about Jim, and I won't have to delve into the depths of my memories to find good things to say about him. Everything about him was good. He didn't have an enemy, and even his Commanding Officer called him 'quite a guy'! He took fellows under his wing—chaps younger and older —any one who felt lost or lonely. They followed him like small puppies. He mothered and brothered them. Men like Jim never die. They always remain with us in the good they have done. And I'd like you to believe what I told my own mother about my brother—Jim will always be watching over you from up there saying, 'Please don't weep in vain. I came to earth to get here. What more happiness could we ask?'"

In the midst of the pain of his own recent loss and the strain of his own hazardous position at the front, this boy, like thousands of other combat and wounded soldiers, tried to comfort, protect and lift the spirits of his family and of his buddies.

Recrossing the Moselle, on our return trip to headquarters,

General Patton was in a reminiscent mood. He reflected on what we could have done if our armies had had enough gasoline to have continued their sweep across France. Even shipments of gasoline by air, supplementing the tank loads pouring over the roads of France and through Belgium, were not enough to keep us going until our engineers could lay pipe lines. And during this enforced stop the Germans re-grouped, consolidated their positions and made a stand near Aachen and along the Moselle River, thereby increasing our hardships and hazards. He explained that when we are advancing we need gasoline and when we are stopped we need ammunition. We destroy bridges, railroads and rolling stock to stop our enemies, and then we must rebuild and replace them to continue our advance. This is what the army calls logistics, the problem of supply, the answers to which fluctuate like the tides in the Bay of Fundy.

My last morning with the Third Army I attended the briefing exercises and then General Patton walked alone with me to the road where I met Father James O'Neill, who accompanied me on my way from the Third Army to the First. And with Willy, his English bull terrier, the General stood by the roadside as we drove away. Father O'Neill was from Montana and I thought that because he was from the West he would be able to help me agriculturally. I asked him a question about something which I could not identify that I saw growing in a field. He said that he thought the yellow flowers were buckwheat. Later, we learned that they were mustard plants and, after that, Father O'Neill told me he was nervous every time we came upon an unusual tree or plant, and that he was going to suggest that Chaplains be furnished with encyclopedias.

At First Army headquarters, I met General Hodges. Soldierly, gentlemanly and quietly determined, he is a man of few words, and in his discussions of military operations he sounds, with his soft Southern voice, like a doctor discussing surgical operations. While we talked, General Hodges insisted that his Chief of Staff, General Keane, and I take the only two chairs in the van while he sat on his old army trunk, saying it was his favorite seat. With economy of words, he skillfully described the progress of present movements and the process of future ones. He had an engaging little chuckle as he explained maneuvers he had made or intended to make, and it was evident that he spared no effort to be sparing of his men.

Early in the morning, after my arrival at First Army headquarters, General Hodges introduced me to General "Lightning Joe" Collins, commander of the Seventh Corps. General Hodges expressed his warm admiration for General Collins, saying: "Joe is a devout man and a great soldier—a combination that is hard to beat." The General, from New Orleans, is a graduate of West Point's famous Class of 1917, the "Class of Generals." He won the Silver Star for personal bravery in the battle of Guadalcanal, when he went through enemy sniper fire, and he was in the front line with his troops in the capture of the Munda Airport, and led the Allied troops that took Cherbourg.

It was with General Collins that I crossed the Siegfried Line. I got out of the jeep and walked through row after row of iron-spiked cement piles protruding like the dragon's teeth they are called. Cleverly and cunningly camouflaged pill-boxes were located at every conceivable strategic point, some camouflaged by Nature herself, so long ago had they been built. Presumed to be impregnable, many were split wide open to the sky. The iron gates that barred the roads had been blasted from their mammoth supports and the deep ditches and tank traps had been bridged. This line of unparalleled defense ran along the borders of Fortress Germany from the North Sea to the Swiss border. Brushwood and trees cover the pyramidal blocks of parts of the Line and the blocks in the open are grass-green to blend with the fields and meadows. To make the blocks a more formidable obstacle, there were iron stakes in the ground connected by tight-twisted barbed-wire strands. But the fortified concrete igloos which the Germans built in strategic positions have been cracked open or smothered with flame, and the deeply built and widely extended concrete blocks have been overturned and broken.

Thoughtfully looking at the defenses of the Siegfried Line, General Collins said: "I shudder to think of the resistance we should have met with if those fortifications had been defended as the Germans intended to defend them." And I was thinking of what another General told me: that, had it not been for the brilliant exploits of the First Army in eliminating the German forces that were supposed to have defended this Line, its breaching would have been possible only at the cost of thousands upon thousands of then-unexpended American lives. And he said that the General chiefly responsible for this brilliant strategic and practical success was General Collins. I had luncheon with General Collins at his headquarters in an old castle within walking distance of the front lines. In one corner of the usual war-map room there was a big bust turned toward the wall. I asked him who it was, thinking it might have been Bach or Beethoven. He answered, "I don't know—let's look and see," and, turning it around, found it was Hitler!

It was in the Church of St. Cornelius in Kornelimunster that I offered my first Mass on German soil for our American troops. The old German pastor told me he was nervous when first he heard I was coming, and when I arrived I found him on his knees scrubbing the floor. He was anxious to be co-operative and cordial, and together with a professor from the Seminary of Cologne, he served the Mass. A quartet of American doughboys sang an "Ave Maria," and German children sang some hymns.

The church was thronged to the doors and the choir loft was filled to the rafters with soldiers in grimy battle dress. I think the German civilians present were deeply impressed by the devotion of the American soldiers, and amazed to see them praying, for they had been told that all Americans were cruel, bloodthirsty and revengeful. When the Americans had entered that town, only a few days earlier, the old men, women and children dropped to their knees, with sheets and towels in their upraised hands in token of surrender, begging mercy, for they had been told, and believed, that the Americans were there to kill them. Our soldiers had been instructed to be correct but not to show cordiality to the Germans, and except in church they were forbidden to gather with them in groups. On this particular occasion so many hundreds of Germans wished to take advantage of this exception that the church was not large enough to hold them all. As the German civilians knelt in prayer, side by side with our American soldiers, fear of them seemed already to have disappeared from their faces; it was an unforgettably peaceful scene in the midst of war, enemies mingling together before the throne of the Prince of Peace.

CHAPTER VIII

OUR SOLDIERS' FAITH

AT the edge of a picturesque village resting peacefully on the side of a hill, in a little house hidden in a small but dense forest, I met the Commanding General of the First Infantry Division, Clarence E. Huebner. This General has the unusual distinction of having held every rank except Brigadier General, from buck private to Major General, in this same First Division. During his extraordinary career he has been twice wounded and has been awarded the D.S.C. with Cluster and the Silver Star. The First Division is first in more than name and the General is very proud to lead it, and for all his men he has the deepest affection. This Division was the first in France in the last war, when it was commanded by General Summerall, and in this war it was the first to land on three beaches: at Oran in North Africa, under the command of the gallant leaders Terry Allen and Theodore Roosevelt, at Gela in Sicily, and on the "Omaha" beachhead near Cherbourg, under the command of General Huebner. The First Division had been in the front lines for two years and, without one day's rest since landing on the Normandy beaches, had just made the deepest American penetration into Germany, near Aachen.

General Huebner and I drove through short stretches of forest, flat open country and low rolling hills, on my way to say Mass for the troops on the outskirts of the little village of Oberforstbach, about four miles from Aachen. During the drive I saw another part of the vaunted German Westwall and more of the pill-boxes, so completely camouflaged that our advancing troops were mowed down even before they had a chance to realize they were in danger. As the tanks roared up the road they were knocked out as easily as if they were made of tin. Overturned, blackened, shell-pocked and crippled, these American tanks were expressive evidences of the crushing crossfire that belched from these steel-and-concrete miniature fortresses and the German 88's. The wreckage of these tanks seemed incredible to me, for when I had first ridden in them I had felt that nothing in the world could stop them as we plowed through deep ditches, crashed through stone walls and uprooted huge trees.

As our jeep bounced over the uneven road, swerving in ankle-deep mud through the dark, chilly forest, General Huebner talked to me about his men, with especial pride in, and praise for, "John Dough"—the Infantryman. Only the dogged determination to overcome all obstacles, no matter how formidable, had brought the First Division through the defenses of the Westwall to the suburbs of Aachen; only the same determination would bring them to the Rhine and Berlin. But in spite of their successes and endurance, the General cautioned against the tough resourceful foe and warned that the German soldiers, now on their own soil, would fight fiercely every inch of the way, using every tactic in the Prussian military catalogue, because their leaders had instilled in them the belief that "death is preferable to slavery." And every inch of ground so far, he added, had been bought at the cost of priceless American blood, because after we had fought past pill-boxes and through tank gunfire, booby traps and mines staggered and slaughtered us. The Germans used an old defensive-delaying trick—ferociously defending a village, street by street, house by house, and even room by room, at great cost to them and to us, and then suddenly withdrawing.

While the General was talking, there was the sudden, shuddering scream of shells and a dozen soldiers, running single file along the narrow roadway below us, instinctively ducked into a gully. One shell exploded fifty or sixty yards away. The boys lay huddled in the mud for a minute or two, then started off again in their hunched dog-trot. They were some of General Huebner's "John Doughs," coming out of the front lines on their way to Mass. Again and again shells screamed and whistled and the General explained that the boys could tell from the sound that the shells were coming towards them.

When we arrived, I found that the soldiers had set up an altar on the engine hood of a jeep under the shelter of a huge camouflage net, and were sheltering themselves in the trees on a knoll sloping toward Aachen. All during Mass the bombardment continued, fulfilling General Huebner's warning about the stubborn resourceful resistance of the Germans, in bloody contradiction to the optimistic observations of a General who, only the preceding week, had said that on this very day I would be saying Mass in the Cathedral of Aachen! Instead, I saw its magnificent dome and single spire through the haze of smoke billowing from bombings and incessant artillery fire. After Mass, I talked with the officers and men whose lives were to pay the price of the capture of Aachen and the conquest of Germany. I met hundreds of these boys, haggard, worn, dishevelled; their faces tattooed with gunpowder and grimy with dust, their uniforms ripped and caked with mud. In appearance, there was nothing heroic about these sad, silent men, but heroes they were, for after days of bitter, grueling fighting they had just captured the key town of Stolberg. Without a single

day's respite, without hot food or drink, they had been in action
for three terrible weeks, and being with them made me realize
the full truth of General Huebner's remark that ninety-nine
percent of his men deserved medals, for I have seen the tragic
spoil of lives and limbs that war has taken as its toll. Science
in its wonder work has learned to replace man's legs and arms
and hands. But science cannot make life's rich red blood
flow through ersatz bone and flesh and make man whole
again.

Tank Gunner Ralph Brown, twenty-five-year-old Corporal
of Youngstown, Ohio, was one of those whose two legs and left
arm were part payment on the gigantic installment plan of war's
total cost in lives and bodies. On German soil he left them,
bloody symbols of his sacrifice for us and for generations yet
unborn. Returned home, every need of his will be fulfilled—
except the need to walk and run again, play and work again
as God made man to do; and all that science can ever accom-
plish will fall far short of what Nature did when this boy was
created straight, strong, stalwart and integrate. At twenty-five,
men yearn for love and family. At twenty-five, thousands of our
men will carry their yearning buried within themselves, yet
every beat of their hearts will be a silent cry of lonely longing,
and no compassion in our own hearts will heal the hurt in
theirs.

In our battle for Germany, one boy who paid a price to him
far greater than his own life was Jim Krebs, also from Ohio.
Jim and Jack were nineteen-year-old twins—an inseparable,
deadly bazooka team—twins who through this war ate, slept,
planned and fought together, as together they had lived before
the war. But they did not die together. Jack died in Jim's arms
and Jim lives with a broken but still fighting heart. I feel that

Jim's letter to his mother may help to console other sonless mothers in their unhealing hurt and hunger.

"Dearest Mom and Dad: You can bet that Jack wasn't any coward. Even to the last he kept his courage, love and faith in God. Well, anyhow, Mom, we were moving up just before dawn, somewhere south of ——, when all hell broke loose. We got pinned down in a river bed with machine guns firing from three directions. As day broke, our position was revealed and they let us have it with mortars, 88's and machine guns. We were forced to make a frontal attack on a machine-gun nest in a stone house.

"Jack and I threw in three bazooka rounds and then took off in the attack. Jack was running to my right front and suddenly he dropped. I hit the ground and crawled over to him. He was unconscious, but I was able to bring him around. He recognized me and smiled. God heard his prayer and took him to a far better place than here on earth. He suffered very little, Mom, we can thank God for that. He died quietly in my arms.

"I started dragging him off the field when a mortar shell landed close and shrapnel got me. It was very slight and I got to a house where an aid station was already set up.

"Mom, Dad—if there was only something I could do to lessen your sorrow, my own grief wouldn't hang quite so heavy on my heart.

"Whenever the going got tough, Jack and I always put our faith in God to bring us through. I remember when we were pinned down all day by enemy machine-gun fire up in Belgium. Eight of us lay there practically freezing and only four of us lived to crawl off the field after dark. All that day, all that night I prayed and I know Jack did too, and that night God kept His protective arms about us. Now with Jack gone, I am alone and lost and nothing can console me except my faith in God, for I know He will help me to do whatever is right."

When the leaders of men throughout the world place their faith in God as Jim did, to guide them to do what is right, then those who must follow will not again be led to destruction and death. It is each man's duty to put *himself* right and keep *himself* in peace, before he can make a peace for others. He must not seek his own glory, for, "Glorious men are the scorn of wise men, the admiration of fools, the idol of parasites and the slaves of their own vaunts," and of such men wars are born!

On my way to visit a medical-aid station of the Twenty-Sixth Regiment, I passed convoy trucks filled with men returning from the front lines. They sat huddled together, leaning against and supporting one another while some of them slept; others, wearily smoking, sat and just stared as they jolted along. One of the unshaven, heavy-eyed solitary lads was playing a mournful hill-billy tune on a harmonica. All were packed in together, all had the same thoughts, yet each was alone with his own.

That entire afternoon I spent with the wounded. Germans as well as Americans, covered and caked with mud, blood dripping from their hastily bandaged wounds, limbs distorted and bones protruding, were brought into the aid station where all were given expert attention. There were not enough cots on which to put all the litters, and as they were taken from the ambulances some of them had to be placed on the ground. Sometimes there are not even enough litters, and one boy with a bad body wound, stricken by the utter helplessness of his buddies, cried out: "*I can walk!*" He raised himself and painfully but pridefully staggered towards the hospital so that his litter might serve some one more broken than he!

In only a few minutes after their arrival the wounded received an infusion of blood plasma, a sprinkle of sulfanilamide, a hypo of morphine, and everything that could help to save their lives, relieve their pain or give them comfort. Some of the boys were drowsy under opiates, some were pathetic and bewildered, others calm and self-possessed. One of these boys, drained pale from loss of blood, whispered his contentment at seeing me and said, "I tried to get to your Mass in Notre Dame, Father, but I had to get back to the front."

With one of the doctors, I threaded my way through the narrow spaces between rows of wounded. Softly he told me a bit about each boy. Cautiously lowering his voice to a bare whisper, he said, "That youngster two litters away just lost both his legs." And the boy lying at our very feet, smilingly spoke up, and my throat tightened as he said, "No, Father, I'm the one who lost both my legs! I'm one of Archbishop Cantwell's boys." He knew that would mean to me that his home was in Los Angeles. I promised that I would tell the Archbishop about him, and I knew that one of the first things I would do on reaching home would be to give him an account of the shining bravery of that youngster.

Some wounded become so battle-fatigued, battle-sick and homesick that they would rather die than go into battle again, while others crave word from the doctors permitting them to return to the front lines. One man, tormented by terrifying memories, said to me with a grim smile on his unsmiling face, "After what I've seen them do to my buddies, I could spend the rest of my days killing Germans." Another boy, frayed with death but unafraid to die, who at twenty had lived longer than a lifetime, pressed my hands and said tranquilly, "I'm all set, Father; I've done my part. The more I have travelled over the world, the more I realized that nothing counts but God. I am ready."

There was another wounded soldier whom I shall long remember. He called me to his cot-side. His eyes, face and voice were pleading as he propped himself up on his two hands and asked: "Father, what's this all about? It's awful, terrible and terrifying. I don't understand it. This morning, I killed eleven Germans! The last one hit me and I lost my leg, but I got him right in the center of his forehead. It's kill or be killed! I'm not of your religion, but I too was taught, and brought up to believe, 'Thou shalt not kill.' Women and children came out of their houses waving sheets and towels, begging us not to kill them. The little children especially got me, because I have two babies of my own. These tiny tots thought we wanted to kill them, while all I wanted to do was to take them in my arms. Tell me what *is* this disease of fury and death?"

This soldier needed no discourse on patriotism. He was patriotism incarnate. Before Pearl Harbor he had enlisted as a Private in the Army and had become a First Lieutenant in the Infantry, and on his blood-stained tunic were the decorations of the Silver Star, the Bronze Star and the Distinguished Service Medal. His violent earnestness pressed me. Like hundreds of thousands, this boy was hungering for an answer and I told him the story of another man who, like himself, yearned to bring peace to a crucified world, a man who could have chosen a career and a life that might have brought him fortune's fame, for he was the son of a successful merchant. Instead, he became a Trappist monk, a member of an Order whose rules are among the most rigid of all religions. Why? "In order to bring God to men and men to God," he said, "to pray for a world that will not pray, to bring back peace to all mankind."

I told him, too, the tale of the very young son of a prominent physician in France, accused of collaboration with the Allies during the German occupation, condemned to be executed as a hostage after a year's internment in a fortress prison. Refusing any defense before the German military tribunal, he said: "I did my duty as a Frenchman. I am your enemy. I ask no favors." In his last letter, he wrote: "Adored Family: I am going to be shot at noon. My testament is brief: I adjure you to keep faith. And mind, no hatred for those who shoot me. 'Love one another' is a Commandment of the religion to which I have returned, and from which you must not deviate. It is a religion of love."

What is the answer? I gave the soldier the only answer that I know, incomprehensible though it may be to war-warped minds and hate-hardened hearts: "Thou shalt love the Lord thy God with thy whole heart and thy whole soul and thy neighbor as thyself." One need not be a Trappist monk, nor one of our world's martyred, to follow this first Commandment. It is as fundamental to an enduring peace as it is to true religion, and those who violate it are the enemies of peace. And until all peoples of this war-racked, war-wrecked, bleeding world learn this lesson of war, and believe and live this Commandment, so long will millions of boys, pitifully pleading, ask, "What is this all about?" as, in the morning of their lives, death comes!

Every day, men also ask of me: "Will religion change in the post-war world? What will be the future of religion in Germany?" To these questions, too, I know only one answer, though many people do not want to believe nor do they even want to hear it. Yet it is the only real answer. It is God's own answer and promise, "Come back to Me and I will come back to you."

The future of religion in Germany is no different from the

future of religion in any other land or the future peace of that land. Blueprints for peace, for world reconstruction, for rehabilitation are many, long, varied and complicated, but there is only one blueprint for the future of Germany and the world. God drew that blueprint! Men of every nation have tried to live by its contradiction and have sown and reaped devastation, destitution and death almost unto the complete destruction of civilization and Christianity. Why, then, will not men try this simple formula for peace that He gave so long ago: Love thy God and love thy neighbor as thyself!

No one has better lived and taught this truth than Cardinal Faulhaber of Munich, from its beginnings one of Nazi-Totalitarianism's mightiest challengers, who, fearlessly outspoken, actively anti-Nazi, begged of his people and priests to remain faithful to their religion and to humanity, and thus to themselves and to God. His own life in jeopardy, the Cardinal, at the height of Nazi domination, pleaded not alone for Catholicism, but for the very life of Christianity. "The Church must stand together in the fight for its existence," he said. "Today, it is a question of life or death for Christianity, for in its blind rage against religion, the Nazi 'faith' does not distinguish between Protestantism and Catholicism." And during the years, Germany has come to know the power of justice and to feel the crunching devastation of the deluge of Allied bombs destroying her people, her lands, her homes. All that might have been spared had her stony-hearted, stubborn-minded leaders accepted the inevitableness of her defeat. And in the fury of these bombings, one by one, most of the churches of Germany collapsed, and Cardinal Faulhaber said that, in Munich alone, forty-three churches lay in utter ruin, making it impossible to have services in any one of them. And, one by one, his priests, too, were imprisoned for no other reason than openly and fearlessly fighting to safeguard religious education and religious freedom.

When first he heard the air-raid signals that presaged the doom of his own beautiful cathedral, the seventy-six-year-old Cardinal was saying the Rosary with members of his household in an underground chapel in Munich. "At four o'clock in the morning, with houses burning and time bombs exploding all around me," the Cardinal said, "I finally reached the cathedral. The sacristy was already wholly ablaze and none of its contents could be saved. High-explosive bombs had smashed the vault above the choir and had even decapitated supporting pillars. The entire sanctuary with its famous choir stalls and the episcopal throne fell prey to the flames. Even three days after the disaster, and despite efforts of the guards on duty, the 'sacrificial fires' broke out again and again. When I stepped from the ruins into the transepts of the cathedral, weeping, praying men and women stretched out their faithful hands to me. Faith in God is resurrection, and many who faltered, failed and left the Church in the 1930's have now returned to religion and to God."

Another great and courageous soldier of God is Martin Niemoeller, who, from the time when Hitler became master of Nazi Germany, daily risked his life for the principles of Christianity in which he believed, for which he fought and because of which he spent eight years in Nazi concentration camps. Pastor Niemoeller was imprisoned because he dared to disobey, and steadfastly led his people to disobey, the Nazi commandment: "Turn from God and obey Hitler."

On the very day of his release, anti-God, anti-freedom-respecting Nazis, who had failed to force him to betray God for Hitler, were taken prisoners by the Allies! And on that first day of Martin Niemoeller's liberation from captivity his message of warning and guidance was: "Turn again to God." Men who suffer for their faith, their beliefs, their God know the depth and the truth of the only answer in which lies the key to the future of religion in Germany and to the future of the world; "Come back to Me and I will come back to you."

Religion does not change. It is the people who have changed. Seared by greeds, they have become geared to a fantastic material pitch, cruelly causing and exploiting one another's miseries. This is the disease, deep-rooted within ourselves, that is slaughtering mankind, and the only cure for this disease is a return to God.

During the battle for Germany, in an aid station hastily set up within shattered walls that were once a house, the bodies and blood of the wounded and dying flooded the floor. Despite their craze of pain, they cried out for the Chaplain to pray for them. Some, clutching their rosaries as if they were holding life within their very hands, and who could only with agony open their bandaged mouths, begged and yearningly received the Bread of Life, while whistling shells and roaring artillery sang their incongruous faith-mocking battle music.

It is true that in war the overwhelmed hearts of soldiers turn more readily to God and that war's terrifying trial and the heart's deep longing for peace compel all men to lean on His comforting power. But I do not believe our boys turn to Him through fear only, or "for the duration." I believe that they who turned to God in the midst of the untold tortures of war will in peacetime cling to Him in gratitude and love.

Until I stood among our dying, where the very air was swollen with surges of seething suffering, I had not realized the agonizing that man endures before life is drained from him. Involuntarily, I would grind my teeth and clench my fists trying to help the wounded bear their pain, as the low moans of the mashed and mangled, an occasional sob from the lonely, the murmurs of doctors and medics tending and soothing their men composed a delirious unfinished symphony of the world's madness!

Countless are the stories of the stanchness, valor and sacrifice, of the superhuman deeds and endurances of our American soldiers. One young Lieutenant—characteristic of so many thousands—had just finished a letter to "Dearest Mom and Dad." The boy's courageous spirit, his concern to lighten the load on his parents' hearts, was as easy to read in his expressive eyes as it was in the pencilled lines:

"In Germany I ran into a little trouble, Mom. I lost my right leg and left foot. This I know will be a shock to you. However, I am your son, and my heritage from you has prepared me to meet this challenge.

"They tell me here in the hospital that in time I shall walk again, and without a limp, after I get the artificial 'businesses.' A new life is ahead of me. It presents new problems and a challenge to see how bravely and sanely I can meet them, and I know I can—with God's help and yours.

"I am in fine spirits. Please do not you be sad."

Most of these boys, in fulfillment of their pledge of allegiance, gave, for us, all that they were or ever hoped to be; and many of them rose to heights of greatness while the unleashed fury of the Nazis lashed out against them. What are we pledging ourselves to give them in return for their lives and limbs, their hopes and dreams, their future that they gave for us? With prayer in my heart I watched men who, no longer able to fight physically, were still fighting morally and spiritually to re-enrich their mutilated minds and bodies, emptied by endless days and nights of front fighting.

Among these boys, and in the midst of these experiences, one of my sharpest memories was of the Union Station in Washington not many months before: a long line of lean, lanky lads—typical American boys—all dressed much alike in their brown, blue and grey sweaters, with slacks that did not match, capless and coatless, identification tags hanging from their buttonholes, all carrying their little bags, all trying to look jaunty and nonchalant and older than their eighteen years. Why did I remember these particular boys? Because passing them was another long line of lean, lanky lads—typical Americans—all dressed alike too, except that many were armless, others legless, some sightless, and all, as they guided one another awkwardly in their new helplessness, were also trying to look nonchalant. The span of actual years between the boys in those two lines could not have averaged more than five, but in experience that span was a lifetime. And the bridge between the lines was war!

One line was on its "way over," and as these boys looked at the others who had just "come back," they paled, and some looked aghast, as if they could not trust their eyes, while others looked away carelessly but intentionally, and all tried to be indifferent. Replacements! A soldier for a soldier. For what were they to do battle? For new frontiers on foreign soil? To replenish the fuel of war? I pray not, but to rekindle the flame of faith; to regain spiritual frontiers; to quench the fires of war and restore men to peace. Nations can be reborn, cities can be rebuilt, spirits and hopes can be revived, and even broken bodies can be rehabilitated, but never will there be the rebirth on earth of one lost life. The dead belong to God, and unless the living of all nations, great and small, powerful and weak, learn the lessons of war, "replacements" will go on long after a "peace" is declared.

Through days and nights I heard the constant grumbling of

artillery fire, the singing and crashing of German shells, and saw the flashing and splashing of our own. One night, under cover of darkness and fortified with a password, but feeling more fortified by the company of two comforting M.P.'s, I went to visit an outfit under the command of General Howell. The password was funny, but I knew it would not be funny if we forgot it! There was not even a ribbon of light. We groped through the darkness, hand in hand, and finally reached our destination, a dimly lighted cellar where we found the General. In the hubbub of noises, General Howell did not understand the officer who introduced us. He took one glance at me, turned to my companion and asked: "Does he speak English?"

I had never before, inside or out, heard so much noise, nor seen so many people working in such a small space, yet everyone except myself knew exactly what he was doing and what was happening every minute. The General had his full quota of equipment, including the inevitable war maps, but this was the first headquarters I had visited where I was more interested in how I was going to get back than in the General's explanation of where his troops were and where they were going!

Early the next morning I said Mass for a group of our soldiers in a division of the First Army commanded by Major General Louis Alec Craig, younger brother of four-starred General Malin Craig, and a great and devout soldier. My vestments were camouflaged and a camouflaged net was stretched above the portable altar. All during Mass intermittent bursts from machine guns broke the continuous rumble of artillery fire, and the soldiers, who often use their helmets for seats, kept them on their heads except at the Consecration. These helmets serve many purposes, from water basins to baptismal fonts; the light pith helmets which cushion the steel ones are used as sun helmets, and occasionally they have been used as collection baskets and filled with coins to help repair a damaged church, hospital or orphan asylum.

CHAPTER IX

THIS PEACE MUST LAST

W ITHOUT leaving the First Army, whose front extended
through France, Belgium, Holland, Luxembourg and
Germany, I continued on my way to Belgium, and I
thought of one soldier who claimed the world's courting record
because, stationed in Germany, he was engaged to a nurse on
duty in Holland, and every time he called on her he had to travel
through three countries. The Belgians greeted us gratefully and
even gaily, though one could sense that their new joy was but
slowly seeping through the century-old fear of the Germans,
who so often and so ruthlessly had invaded their soil. Homemade
American flags flew from many of their houses, and though some
were short in the number of stripes, and all were short in the
number of stars, these flags were pleasant to see, for they reflected the good-will of the people and their hope in us for happiness. Along the roadways were signs: "For you, Americans, Beer
and Lemonade," and, "We give our hearts to the American people as souvenirs of our liberation." In the town of Eupen, one of
the towns taken from Germany and given to Belgium by the
Treaty of Versailles, a clothesline stretched across a street with the
sign "Siegfried Line," and hanging from it was an effigy of Hitler. We drove through cities and villages and through apple and
plum country, where one could actually pick the fruit without
being killed by booby traps, for the Germans had had no time
to hang them, as they did in Italy, 'midst dusty grapes and ripen-
ing figs.

In a château in which I stayed, the people wanted to know whether the Americans would remain in Belgium to protect them after the war. That night I was in favor of it, if only out of gratitude for a good night's sleep in a bed which must have been like the one in which Little Red Riding Hood's grandmother had slept. One had to jump, or else climb on a little stool, to get into it. As good as the bed looked to me, it looked even better to Father Stephen Kenny, who was with me, for it was the first one he had even seen in four months. Before we went to sleep he told me about one of the Chaplains, who had made the mistake of being the first American to enter a certain Belgian town. He had not realized that he was ahead of the patrols, and found himself just behind the retreating Germans. The people came cautiously out of their houses, some with upraised hands, many waving towels and handkerchiefs, trying to surrender to him! There were tears in the eyes of the old and cheers in the voices of the young when they realized they were liberated. Bells rang out, and jubilantly the Belgians flocked to church, where they offered a Mass of thanksgiving for their freedom and sang hymns and their national anthem.

In Belgium, I heard the same kind of disturbing, distressing stories that I had heard both in liberated and unliberated countries; stories of hatred and distrust among co-nationals and even between neighbors and members of the same family. In some instances these have become as deep and bitter as the hatreds against foreign aggressors and oppressors, and while we need not be alarmists we must be alarmed, for war's virus has poisoned human bloodstreams, infecting minds and hearts, dividing peoples whose common interests and destinies should unite them! But my heart was consoled by one story of great faith, loyalty and devotion. In a small Belgian town, for more than four years an old priest harbored a dozen Jewish children. He provided for them out of his own resources, helping to care for their physical and spiritual needs as best he could. On his calendar he marked their Sabbath and holy days, and many refugees and American servicemen observed their holy days in his house. On the Day of Atonement, so that they might not leave his roof hungry after their fast, he spent all that day collecting food for them. Not only the very young, but also the very old, were of his brood and came under his compassionate protection, and hundreds of refugees with his aid escaped from the Gestapo. Finally, the Nazis became suspicious and the priest had to go into hiding, but first he secured the children's safety in the rectory of another church. When the town was liberated he returned and again took into his care stranded, homeless Jewish children and arranged for their adoption by Jewish families.

In Charleroi, I visited an armory which had been converted into a prison for alleged collaborationists accused of traffic with the enemy. Women, wives, mothers and sisters, with anguished faces, hovered around the jail, their tear-brimmed eyes clinging plaintively to the barred windows, while they waved frantically towards the grim brick walls in the hope that their loved ones might see them through the narrow slits in the masonry. I had no knowledge of the guilt or innocence of the imprisoned, but some of the relatives were strong in asserting that the only crime of their dear ones was that they had not been killed by the Nazis. One Belgian merchant wryly observed, "It's impossible to differ even slightly with any one without running the danger of being shot, and that's the only way to have the last word in an argument."

From the fevered, faltering lips of many eye-witnesses I

heard of the cruelty and torture inflicted by the invaders. One Chaplain in the White Army, as the Belgian partisan forces are called, was tortured and had both hands pierced before he was shot by the Nazis. Another priest, a Jesuit, was saturated with gasoline and thrown into a fire. Fortunate were they who died from a head-shattering or a chest-piercing bullet, in comparison with those whose lives were leached by torture practiced by some of the world's worst sadists. So revolting and diabolical are the atrocities that were deliberately inflicted on innocent civilians throughout Europe, that unless there was evidence substantiating the facts these tales would be unbelievable!

Here, and in many other countries, political and religious differences and internal rancors have impeded national unity and deflated the value of human life. In America, deep as our differences may be and bitter as they can be, they still are settled in courts of law in accordance with the principles of law. In America, minorities have the protection of the law and all Americans have the obligation to protect every citizen in all his civic rights. And woe betide America if disunion, dishonesty, greed, violence and corruption knock down and undermine the foundation of her stability and greatness!

My first stop in Holland was in Mastrich, a city I had known in peacetime. It still appeared neat and clean, and the red-white-and-blue horizontal-striped flag of the Netherlands flew from every home, even though every home and heart has been broken by the horror of Nazi invasion. One old Hollander, weeping, said of our boys, "Their smiling faces, their kindness, their generosity and especially their simplicity have won our hearts, and deep is our gratitude to them." Almost every family in this small country was undernourished, and the women and children live in cruel fear for their men abducted by the Nazis and forced into slave labor within the danger zones.

In Holland I was the guest of General Charles Corlett, known to all the Army by his nickname, "Pete." The last place we had met was in Alaska, and in the meantime he had become one of the heroes of Guadalcanal. When I mentioned the mud through which we had jeeped our way to find him, he reminded me that it was nothing as compared to Alaskan mud. But it did not cheer the soldiers slogging their way day after day through Holland to know that somewhere else the mud was thicker and deeper!

"Pete" told me about Captain Rooney of New York, Field Artillery Chaplain, whose specialty in the war seemed to be caring for the tiniest folk. He was driving through one town when the enemy began to pound the road with shells. Running to take shelter, Chaplain Rooney saw a frightened little girl crouched in the very middle of the road. The shells were hitting so close to the youngster that he thought she would be hit before he could cover the half-block to reach her. He took the child in his arms, covered her completely with his stooped body and got safely to a shelter. From sheer relief, the youngster began to cry and the Chaplain started to console her. Suddenly, he began to laugh. The child immediately forgot her fears and laughed too. The story that prompted the Chaplain's laugh, and turned the psychological trick, was his recollection of an American youngster whom he had once tried to soothe by saying: "I wouldn't cry that way if I were you," and the little girl had answered: "This is the way I cry; you can cry the way you want to!" During another bombardment, Chaplain Rooney heard a mother cry out wildly that her baby was alone on the top floor of the house. He ran through the shelling, got the baby and carried her to safety. Awarded the Silver Star "for unselfish devotion to humanity," the Chaplain said: "'Tis nothing—just the luck of the Irish."

But I know it is not luck but great-spirited courage that makes many Chaplains and each boy a hero. One boy, both of his legs blown off, both hands mangled, with mortar shells crashing around him, cried hoarsely to his comrades, "Get into your holes; don't worry about me!" A Chaplain raised the boy in the cradle of his arms, prayed and gently talked to him. "I want terribly to live," the youngster whispered, "but if God wants me, I am ready." Then, with utter simplicity and faith, he asked God to save from pain and death as many as He could, to bless every one, everywhere, "and the enemy too," he breathed softly, "for they know not what they do." He died. The doctor, with tear-filled eyes—eyes accustomed daily to seeing boys gutted, ravaged and torn—turned to the Chaplain and said: "After that, it is not hard to believe in God. I am humbled, for I have seen the glory of God reflected in this boy!"

Another story, tinged with a twist of humor, was told by a Chaplain who spent Christmas afternoon with the boys at the front, visiting them in their foxholes, ministering to their physical and spiritual comfort. A nineteen-year-old doughboy asked him if it was too late to make his First Communion. "It's never too late and there never will be a better day," the Chaplain answered, and jumped into the foxhole. The communicant, being a good soldier, kept one eye on the Chaplain, one eye on a German machine gun across No Man's Land, and one finger on the trigger of his gun!

Driving through grief-worn, war-weary Belgium, I saw many of her famous, graceful cities bearing gaping, disfiguring war wounds and I met many of the afflicted of those cities, also worn and war-wounded. I talked with some of Belgium's brave Underground fighters, who had fought fiercely from the Ardennes to the Lys, and I visited their devotional center hidden deep within the beautiful Ardennes. Steps of beaten earth led to its rustic altar, and the statues were carved from the trees of the forests. During the years of occupation and oppression, village priests in jute paratroop uniforms crept silently through the woods to celebrate Mass for the Resistance troops. From one of them, I heard a story that portrayed the supreme devotion of the Belgian people to their God, to their country and to the men who fought and died to preserve it. These men are a bold challenge to the Godless who, in their conquests, captured and crushed men's bodies but never their great souls. A village priest, watching from his garden, saw a powerful formation of American bombers roaring through the heavens, returning to their bases from a raid on Germany. One of the Liberators appeared to be in difficulty, and black smoke trailed the limping plane. Suddenly, four parachutes appeared in the sky. But one of them did not open! As it plummeted earthwards, the priest, in dread anticipation of death, gave absolution as he ran into the meadow towards the fallen parachuter. The boy was still breathing, and reverent hands lifted him and carried him to a nearby house. A thin trickle of blood was oozing from a wound which appeared to be only a scratch on the boy's head, and the priest hoped prayerfully for life. But before the doctor reached the boy's side, the lad was dead. His skull had been fractured in the crash.

The Mayor and the villagers wanted to bury this boy with military honors, but when the German officers arrived they even refused to permit the priest to bless his grave! But the Belgians, in their Christian revenge against this cruel, stupid irreverence, thronged to the parish church, where Masses were offered throughout the days for the fallen American aviator. This was a tribute of affection and gratitude that the Germans could not prevent, nor did they know that one little old lady had dared quietly and gently to slip a simple signet ring from the boy's finger and give it to the priest, some day to send to his mother. And I know that now this ring has begun its journey home!

In Belgium, Holland and Germany, I saw German prisoners of various types and under various conditions, some isolated in wards in our large military hospitals, others, in field tents, lying side by side with our own wounded, receiving identical treatment from our doctors, nurses and medical personnel. Nearly all of these prisoners were physically exhausted, nerve-shattered, listless and hopeless. Drained of arrogance and relieved to be captured, to me they seemed surprised and bewildered at the humane treatment they received. Five members of one prisoner's family had been killed in the bombing of Hamburg, and one of them was his two-year-old daughter. When he was told that when the war was over he would be returned to Germany, he answered, "I never want to see Germany again. There, I suffered sorrow, hunger and disease; I knew fear; I saw mutilation and slaughter; I lived in mud and blood. I am dying to die!"

In a little village near Aachen, I passed a column of about five hundred German prisoners, some very young and some very old, among them a small group of fanatical SS. troops and a dozen ramrod-straight stern Prussian officers, still defiant and confident that Germany would win, even while the crunching vise of war was crushing her to death. There were others, crumpled, collapsed, entirely bereft of their combat spirit, stragglers who had surrendered to our medicos. Expressionless children and hausfraus stood by the gates of their homes and quietly wept or tried to smile, as these prisoners marched to a collecting point to be trucked to prisoner-of-war camps. They tossed apples, pears or schwarzbrot to the men, and the hunger-bitten prisoners ate fiercely.

The Nazis tried to weaken the morale of our American prisoners of war by circulating propaganda that because our soldiers had been captured they were cowards. But I know that none of them were cowards and that many of them were heroes forced to surrender and to accept a captivity of gnawing loneliness, of living death and sometimes of sudden death. One courageous, beloved soldier, Major General Maurice B. Rose, gave bitter public proof of this when he was ruthlessly shot by the Germans while being taken prisoner.

I had promised to say Mass in Luxembourg for our soldiers of the Fifth Corps commanded by Major General Leonard Gerow. Bad weather prevented us from flying and we had to drive three hours over mud-clogged, rain-beaten roads. It was cold and windy, with rain turning to sleet and hail, and then turning back again to pelting rain. Passing from Germany into Luxembourg, I drove through the town of Spa, where Hitler had had his headquarters. It was also in Spa, during the first World War, that the Kaiser learned from General von Hindenburg that there was no longer any hope of saving Germany from defeat. It was not strange that my thoughts refused to stay with today, but flashed back to disasters past, and forward to the problems and dangers of tomorrow. I thought of our boys, conditioned for war by months of rigid discipline, tedious, timeless testing and training. Their bodies had been tempered to withstand the rigors of extreme weather and of foxhole living, habituated to sleepless days and nights and alerted to combat. Their hands were readied to the tools of war; their feet hardened to mount guard on a lonely sentry post, to make forced marches or keep a rigid battle-stance when the slightest movement would mean death. Thus were they conditioned for war.

But what, I wondered, of the conditioning of these millions of fighting men for peace? When the guns cease firing, are we prepared to train these men for the tasks of conserving the peace with the same realism and vigor with which they were trained for war? Are we prepared to develop men's minds towards peace with the same intensity with which we disciplined men's bodies for war? Will we guide and equip them for the pace of peace with the same determination with which we geared them to the pace of war? Will we forge the links in the chain for peace with the same ardor with which we forged the links in the chain for war? Will leaders of nations continue to try to establish and enforce peace by decree from above, instead of building the foundation for an enduring peace upon the mutual understanding, good-will and well-being of the families and communities who gave their sons to war?

In war, Americans of every race, creed and color were worthy to be sent to fight and die and be buried side by side. In peace, shall we forget too soon the inglorious indignities wrought by man upon man, the lavish loss and wanton waste of cherished lives, the destruction of cities, the desolation of lands and nations, the degradation of moral and spiritual values?

We have already begun the process of forgetting if we think that peace will come by formulas, covenants or decrees, that peace means only the re-construction of devastated areas and the revival of trade; or that peace is propaganda, for mere words and phrases are no more tools of peace than they are the implements of war. Down through the centuries, bloody battles have been fought all over the world, but it is sad and ominous that the countries which boast they have made the greatest contributions to civilization are those which have excelled in the vengeance and violence of war. To win the battles of peace we need the same determination and tactical genius that are needed to win the battles of war. Men must be conditioned for the pursuits of peace with the same steadfastness and perseverance with which they were disciplined for combat in war, and training for a permanent peace can be achieved at a fraction of the cost of preparing for periodic wars!

Driving through so many towns whose names stud our history books was like taking an Alice-in-Wonderland trip, except that today it is a trip through blood-sweat-and-tears land. I have heard it said in sad cynicism that the greatest punishment for Mussolini and Hitler would have been to have made them listen to their own and to each other's speeches. But one punishment, I believe, would have exceeded all others: to have forced them to retread the paths they have drenched in blood, to stand among the ravages and ruins of proud cities they have gored and see the hollowed shells of once-hallowed homes of worship and of love, to heed the sick, the maimed, the broken and bereaved, *to watch the children!* and, in the wake of all, to look upon the dead—the luxuriant youth laid waste by them!

When we finally reached the woods of Luxembourg, I found awaiting me two thousand boys unmindful of the hail and driving rain. A sheet of canvas strung from four trees covered the improvised altar within the forest but afforded little protection, and my vestments and the boys' uniforms were drenched by the water which literally streamed down our bared heads and faces. A band played the soft, soul-stirring strains of "Ave Maria," and I was inspired, as always I have been throughout the world, by the faith of our men of the front lines, so humble and sincere.

After Mass, talking with the boys, sharing hot coffee and dough-
nuts distributed from Red Cross Clubmobiles, we heard the
thunder and rumble of artillery, and only then did we realize
that, strangely, there had been no shelling during the entire
service!

Again I was on my way. On the main Aachen-Liège highway,
I stopped at a new American cemetery, stretching across a wide
wind-swept field marked off by sparse hedges and crude fences
of fieldstone. On one side, the terrain sloped gently to the
beautiful valley of the Meuse, and on the opposite side there
opened a vista of green fields and low rolling hills dotted with
old farm buildings and even older churches. At a turn in the
road, I lingered at a wayside Calvary erected by the pious farmer-
folk of the region, and said a Rosary for all our dead and their
bereaved belovèd.

Here was a military cemetery in the making, a new sanctuary,
where not only the bodies of our soldiers were being buried but,
with them, the hearts and hopes of those who loved them. Some
day, it too would be trim and well-kept, with tall trees restlessly
moaning and rustling in the wind. Some day, its serried white
Crosses and Stars of David would be set off by freshly raked
gravel paths and cool green lawns, as in Brookwood outside
London, as in the American Cemetery by the lake near Oran,
or as in the one at sun-baked Ponte Olivo looking down across the
plain of Gela toward the lapping blue waters of the Mediterranean. But on this day it was a lonely expanse of sticky black
mud, with yawning holes of familiar shape and depth dug in low
rows lined by white tape.

In one corner, the day's harvest of the dead lay piled. Some
were just as they had come, fresh-fallen from the field of battle,
bloodstained and gory. Some, from the field and evacuation

hospitals, still wore their splints and bandages or dressings, now sadly soiled, disarranged and shaken loose, mute, melancholy evidence of the fervent but vain attempts of medical corpsmen to save them. Others lay wrapped in their mud-spattered, soggy white ducking sacks, which serve as mattresses for the living and as burial shrouds for the dead. Some lay twisted and horribly contorted; some were bloated; some were burned and charred.

Here lay the youth of a "decadent democracy," modern youth accustomed from earliest years to the ease, the comfort, the so-called luxuries of typical American living, yet capable of going out, with an infectious grin, a witty wisecrack and a hasty prayer, and dying for an ideal; dying for the America they knew and loved, dying for lands and peoples unknown to them. Across the swirling, swollen Meuse behind them were the lands they had liberated, where the streets had been thronged with people who greeted them with wild shouts of acclaim, music and laughter, with tears, kisses, handclasps and a torrent of grateful words. They had tasted the brief, exhilarating glory of the liberator and, then, they too had been freed from the bondage of war—forever freed!

On the other side of the farthermost hill lay the land those still living would conquer and, in conquering, liberate from the thralldom of Nazi paganism. I thought of Rupert Brooke and his little corner of the earth that would be forever England. I thought of Alan Seeger and his youthful springtime rendezvous at some disputed barricade. I thought of the gentle, kindly Joyce Kilmer and his trumpet-note of young death floating clear in the wood of Rouge Bouquet. I thought of all the others of that great and youthful host who, so little time ago, had also died to make the world safe for democracy—and for us.

The silence was broken only by the mournful sound of picks

and shovels hacking at the soft yielding earth—gateway to the only peace thousands of our boys, who fought for peace, would ever know. Sad and still, I stood with them in the dank mud while the chill, grey, dripping fog and marrow-searching cold hugged me, and I prayed that love and tolerance may quench the fires of bigotry and of hate and that in their ashes we may plant the seeds of peace.

I looked again upon the stricken, scarred, shocking remains of fun-loving, peace-loving Americans lately turned soldier who, stout-hearted, strong-limbed, vibrant and daring, had fallen facing the foe upon the soil to which they had carried the flag of freedom. Our martyred dead have made our nation consecrate and it falls upon us, the living, to preserve it! Standing with our hallowed, silent dead, the memory of them forever graven within me, I pondered this trust they have laid upon us. Sorrow welled high in my heart, and I understood but this:

No greater love a man can have than this,
That he should lay his life down for his friend—
Now, as I live again the varied scenes
And world-wide pattern of our fighting men,
It seems no other thought so amply fills
The measure of their sacrifice, or plumbs
So well the depth of love that has inspired
Heroic giving of themselves for us.

No greater love than this: it is a truth
Perhaps more deeply lived by some, yet lived
By all the firm and serried ranks of those
Who form a sword of light, a sword of souls,
Forged in the battle-heat of shell and bomb,

Beat out upon the anvil of our need,
Tempered by justice, and in justice drawn
Against a dreadful foe; and though it break,
Yet in its breaking is its mission won—
Even in death. These souls, this sword, shall find
The sheath of final peace, in sacrifice.

Behold the making of this mystic blade:
He was a tiny babe. His sister asked,
"Mother, he is so small, will he grow big?"
The mother smiled and kissed her baby son
Before reply: "Yes, sweetheart, he will grow,
And some day in the shadow of his strength
Many shall rest, even as you and I
Now rest within his father's kindly care."
He was a boy, just one among the throng,
The treasure-trove that is a nation's wealth—
A boy with all a boy's strange wandering ways,
Finding adventure in the fields and woods,
Turning from games to books reluctantly,
Eager to live before he sensed the price
That life would ask of him. How could he know,
As he stood daily at his desk in school,
The spark that he was nursing in his soul—
"I pledge allegiance to my country's flag
And to the principles for which it stands,
One nation, indivisible," he pledged,
"With liberty and justice here for all."
This was the spark of freedom that would grow,
As the boy also grew, in God's good sight.
He found a world without, to which his thoughts

Within, at home, at play with other boys,
Gave glad assent. Too soon his mother found
Her son was child no more. In school, he grew
In knowledge; in the field, at sports he strove
With other boys, he worked to "make the team,"
To win the game, and learn the game of life,
Winning or losing, to play it clean and square—
And learn to win by loss as well as gain.
The boy was growing, to become a man,
Not in the mold of Nazi-Fascist thought,
But in the way America provides
For bodies' growth in strength and minds' in truth.
Then came another dawning time of hope:
As hills become apparent through a mist,
So, vaguely yet, loomed in his heart the dream—
Ideas, ideals, ambitions beckoned him,
Gave impulse to his thoughts; and in those thoughts
Was born resolve to take his rightful place,
A man, with men. Another picture stood
Upon his bureau now, another heart
Took place, beside his mother's, in his own,
And life and love were sweet, and home secure.

December Seventh, Nineteen-Forty-One!
A nation, that had knelt to pray, rose up
Reborn, to meet the challenge of brute force,
And from a million homes, as from the hills
The brooks break forth in spring, the young men came,
Stern-faced. Now in the fire that others lit
The precious ore of lives was forged and shaped
Into the giant blade that, swung athwart

The sky and hurtling o'er the sea, has dealt
A mightier blow, in this dark hour of war,
Than ever yet was struck by men for man.

What fire tempers hearts, what greater flame
Than hate prepared this blade? The flame of Love!
No greater gift the human heart can make
Than life itself. And so in faith we pray
That He who was Himself broken upon
The Cross will gather up and mend forever
These broken blades that we now venerate.
And that is why above the holy sod
Where these blades sheathèd rest, we place with prayer
The symbol of the Greatest Love that men
Have ever known—fired by the Flame Divine,
These found within themselves, by Heaven's grace,
A strength beyond the strength to live, a strength
Which is the strength, for what we love, to die.

Come then, let us not think of these our dead
Save only in the light of Easter morn,
For God with special love embraces those
Whose lives with Him are lived and in Him die.
Truly, in death these dear ones have found Life;
Truly, in Life our martryrs have found peace.

Some say our dead were born expendable;
In this sense only speak they true: There is
No wiser spending of this earthly span
Than, like the Master, greater love to prove
By dying for the cause one holds most dear.

The night breeze moves above our dead to-night,
To-morrow's light with warmth will touch their graves,
Yet none of them so silently shall sleep
But that the angels' lips shall o'er them breathe
The Master's benediction: Greater love
Than this no man can have, that he lay down
His life that other men may live in peace.